To / Ros

# VALIANT HEARTS

## Robin Sharp

*Robin Sharp*

Redbreast Publications

The publication date of 'Valiant Hearts' - 28th June 2019 - has been chosen because this day exactly marks 100 years since the signing of the Treaty of Versailles, which officially brought the First World War to an end.

ISBN 978-0-9535821-1-2

Published by Redbreast Publications
The Blacksmith's Cottage, Drinkstone, Suffolk, UK

Printed by Gipping Press Ltd, Suffolk, UK

*War Memorials, All Saints' Church*

*"A memorial is erected not because of death but because there was a life, a life to be remembered by our children's children's children."* Quote from a local Suffolk stone mason.

# O Valiant Hearts

O valiant hearts who to your glory came
Through dust of conflict and through battle flame;
Tranquil you lie, your knightly virtue proved,
Your memory hallowed in the land you loved.

Splendid you passed, the great surrender made;
Into the light that nevermore shall fade;
Deep your contentment in that blest abode,
Who wait the last clear trumpet call of God.

Long years ago, as earth lay dark and still,
Rose a loud cry upon a lonely hill,
While in the frailty of our human clay,
Christ, our Redeemer, passed the self-same way.

Still stands His Cross from that dread hour to this,
Like some bright star above the dark abyss;
Still, through the veil, the Victor's pitying eyes
Look down to bless our lesser Calvaries.

O risen Lord, O Shepherd of our dead,
Whose cross has bought them and Whose staff has led,
In glorious hope their proud and sorrowing land
Commits her children to Thy gracious hand.

*O Valiant Hearts* is a hymn remembering the fallen of the First World War, that is sung every year during the Remembrance Day service in All Saints' Church, and after which this book has been named. The words were taken from a poem by Sir John Stanhope Arkwright (1872–1954), which was published in *'The Supreme Sacrifice, and other Poems in Time of War'* (1919). It was set to music by Dr. Charles Harris.

# Table of Contents

# Preface

Shortly after moving to Drinkstone in 2004, I attended the annual Remembrance Sunday service in All Saints' Church. The service began with these opening words: *"Let us remember before God and commend to his sure keeping: those who have died for their country in war; those whom we knew, and whose memory we treasure"*. The names of the men on the two village war memorials were then read aloud – fifteen from the First World War and three from the Second. Lines from Laurence Binyon's famous poem 'For the Fallen' were quoted, the last line of which we all ritually repeated: *"We will remember them"*. Last Post was played by the cornets of the Norton Salvation Army band, and we fell silent for 2 minutes.

In that silence, it suddenly struck me that of all those present in a crowded church, very few *could* have known or had personal, treasured memories of those whose names we had just heard, certainly from the First World War, almost 90 years after it had ended. I felt a sudden pang of sadness with the realisation that most of the congregation, including me, knew little more than the name and regiment of the men as inscribed on the stone, and nothing of their lives.

As Reveille sounded, I resolved to try to find out something about each man – where they lived, what they did to earn a wage, who their family, friends and neighbours might have been, how they died. In a way, my aim was to bring back life, colour and substance to mere names and to try to ensure that we did indeed have something to remember them by. The result, partly, is what you now hold in your hand.

Along the way, I gradually uncovered facts and small snippets of information, like an archaeologist slowly scraping away the surface to reveal the treasures below. In turns I have been excited, exhilarated, saddened, amused; I have been in awe and humbled at the conditions and deprivations that these men and their families faced. I will not forget the tingle that went up my spine when I discovered that one of the men, John Whiting, and his family lived in part of the house in which I and my family now live. I imagine him leaving through the front door for work as a gardener at Hessett House, just up the road, or when he bade farewell that final time as he went off to France, where he received the gunshot wound that ended his life.

On occasion, I have felt uncomfortable that I was finding out about facets of lives which perhaps those men might have preferred to keep private, especially bearing in mind the very different outlooks and mores of their times. However, to my mind, there were no awful embarrassments or skeletons in any cupboards and after all, this was partly why I had embarked on the project in the first place – to bring them back to life; this is what made them human. But most of all, I have felt privileged to have looked at these snapshots of their lives and I have emerged with great respect for them all.

And so I have reached the end of this particular journey, that began in All Saints' Church a decade and a half ago. I have arrived via the exhibitions I put together following the Village Hall committee's decision to mark the centenary of the First World War in that way. Fifteen separate exhibitions displayed for one month each, at All Saints' Church and then the Drinkstone War Memorial Institute (Village Hall), to coincide with the 100th anniversary of each man's death.

As yet there have been no public exhibitions to honour the lives of the men on the Second World War memorial – their deaths occurred three-quarters of a century ago. Nonetheless, it is just as important that their stories are told and so they are also included here. I commend all these men to you and through this book we fulfil the solemn pledge: 'We will remember them'.

Robin Sharp, Drinkstone, 28 June 2019

## ABOUT THE AUTHOR

Robin Sharp was born in East Ham, London in 1953. His grandfathers both served in the Great War – Bert Sharp was an observer in the RAF and Frederick Vyse was a Royal Engineers carpenter before secondment to the Royal Tank Regiment. Both returned home safely after the War, but were not unaffected by their experiences. Robin attended East Ham Grammar School for Boys where he developed an interest in the history of the First World War and also performed in a production of 'Oh! What a Lovely War'. After obtaining a BA Honours degree in history and archaeology at the University of Liverpool, he joined the staff of the National Army Museum, Chelsea and worked in the Department of Records from 1981 to 1985. He then changed career and became a charity fundraiser/public relations officer with the RNLI, Save the Children and East Anglia's Children's Hospices. In 2004 he moved to Drinkstone and married his wife Louise. He gave up full time employment in 2006 to care for their two daughters, Ellie and Caitlin. He is a life member of the War Memorials Trust and has served on the management committee of the Drinkstone War Memorial Institute since 2009.

**EAST ANGLIAN DAILY TIMES,**

**FRIDAY, SEPTEMBER 4, 1914.**

### DRINKSTONE.

A meeting was held at the School at Drinkstone on Wednesday evening, at which Colonel Hervey presided, supported by Major Duncan Webb, Mr. A. J. Oxborrow, and Dr. Wood. The speakers were Major Webb and Mr. A. J. Oxborrow, and fourteen recruits volunteered for enlistment, thirteen of whom were accepted.

*Courtesy: Claire and Piers Day*

On 5th August 1914, the day after Britain declared war on Germany, Field-Marshal Lord Kitchener became Secretary of State for War. He decided to raise, by voluntary means, a series of 'New Armies'. A national appeal for volunteers was made on 7th August.  After a slow start, there was a surge in recruiting in late August/early September 1914. In all, 478,893 men joined the army between 4th August and 12th September - 33,204 on 3rd September alone. In fact, the authorities were overwhelmed by the response, finding it difficult to cope with numbers involved.

Feelings of patriotism and a collective sense of duty to King and Empire helped make the appeal successful. Some also enlisted for adventure, others to escape a laborious, dangerous or humdrum job. For instance, life as an agricultural worker at this time was arduous. Many men sought to break away from the daily grind, food shortages, low wages and insecurity by signing up, even before the Great War began. As several volunteers pointed out, by joining the forces they had regular pay and employment, wholesome food several times a day - and clothing was provided.

# FIRST WORLD WAR

IN HONOURED MEMORY OF
THE MEN OF THIS PARISH
WHO GAVE THEIR LIVES IN THE GREAT WAR
1914 — 1918.

THOMAS BARKER. 7TH SUFFOLKS.　ARTHUR PRYKE, CITY OF LONDON.
JAMES CORNISH, SGT 3RD LEICESTERS.　GEORGE ROSE, SGT M.M. 8TH SUFFOLKS.
WILLIAM EDWARDS, ROYAL ENGINEERS.　CECIL ROSE, 8TH SUFFOLKS.
JAMES GILL, 2ND SUFFOLKS.　SYDNEY ROSE, 8TH SUFFOLKS.
ALFRED HARVEY, 6TH YORKS.　HARRY SEELEY, 2ND SUFFOLKS.
WALTER HALLS, 8TH SUFFOLKS.　ALBERT SMITH, 1ST WEST YORKS.
BERTIE PHILLIPS, 3/5TH LEICESTERS.　JOHN WHITING, 8TH SUFFOLKS.
DUNCAN VERE WEBB, CAPT M.C. 1ST LEICESTERS.

Although we know that the Village Hall – Drinkstone's official War Memorial – was in use by early 1922, no records have been traced to provide a date for when the First World War memorial plaque was placed on the north wall of All Saints' Church, or when any official unveiling took place. It measures: 29½" (75cms) high, by 44" (112cms) wide. The earliest reference to the memorial being in the church comes from a newspaper report in the summer of 1934. It is in an account of the wedding of Kathleen Edwards (the daughter of Sapper William Edwards) to Sidney Young ~ (the bride) *"carried a bouquet of blood red carnations, which was afterwards placed near the War Memorial tablet in the church in memory of her father"*.

The search for information continues.....

# JAMES CORNISH

Sergeant, 2nd Battalion Leicestershire Regiment
Army Number 10358
*KILLED IN ACTION 13th March 1915*

The birth of Geoffrey James Cornish was registered in the Thingoe District of Suffolk by his mother, Mildred Sarah Cornish (a domestic servant). His record of birth gives the place as Rougham and a date of 8th April 1890. 'Name and Surname of Father' is left blank.

In the 1891 census, Geoffrey Cornish is listed as being aged 11 months, living with his mother Mildred (a 'charwoman', aged 27) and an older brother, Francis Cornish (aged 4) in Kingshall Green, Rougham. Kingshall Green is on the boundary of Rougham and Bradfield St George, in the area where Bradfield and Rougham Baptist Church is now situated. By the time of the 1901 census, Mildred had married Jeff Catchpole (at Hessett on 16th August 1899) and they were living at Rams Green, Hessett. Geoffrey James Cornish now appears on the census form as James Cornish, aged 10. He is listed alongside two younger siblings, George Cornish, aged 6 years, and Geoffrey Catchpole, aged 6 months. A reason for Geoffrey James Cornish to 'drop' his first name and to be known thereafter just as 'James'?

From a report in the *Bury and Norwich Post* of 22nd May 1900, it would seem that the relationship between James' mother and his stepfather was a stormy one. A case of assault by Jeff Catchpole on (Mildred) Sarah Catchpole was heard (but dismissed) at Thingoe and Thedwastre Petty Sessions, but not before witnesses had declared that the parties involved were 'generally quarrelling'.

Against this background, maybe the youthful James would have been content to leave the parental home. In any case, on 16th February 1909 James joined the army reserve in Bury St Edmunds as a member of the 3rd Battalion of the Leicestershire Regiment, signing up, initially at least, for 6 years' service. He gave his trade as 'gamekeeper' and, indeed, in the 1911 census he is recorded as an 'under gamekeeper', boarding with Frederick Simkin, gamekeeper (presumably for the Rougham Estate) in Norton Road, Thurston.

According to the Army Attestation Form that James signed, his declared age was 18 years and one month old (though this doesn't quite add up, as it would have made his date of birth January 1891 rather than April 1890). Several personal details are recorded: he was 5'7" tall, weighed 125 lbs (8 stone 13 lbs), had reddish brown hair and grey eyes, with a slightly different shade in each eye; his chest measurement was 31" increasing to 33½" when fully expanded; his pulse rate was 76. A small scar was noted on the back of his left hand. In addition, four vaccination marks were recorded on his left arm, carried out in 'infancy', but notwithstanding, he was re-vaccinated on the 1st March.

Over the next five years James Cornish attended various training courses and camps – for instance a musketry course from 12th August to 11th September 1910, followed immediately by 'Annual Training' between 12th and 26th September. How his employers felt about his 6½ week absence from gamekeeping activities we do not know, but perhaps they accepted it as James Cornish carrying out his patriotic duty. Cornish began his service as a private, of course, but progressed steadily through various promotions: lance corporal from 5th June 1911, corporal from 29<sup>th</sup> July 1912 and finally he was appointed sergeant on 4<sup>th</sup> September 1914.

When war was declared on 4<sup>th</sup> August 1914, as a reservist, James Cornish was quickly mobilised. After initial training with the 3<sup>rd</sup> Battalion Leicestershire Regiment, based at Fort Purbrook, near Portsmouth, he was assigned to the 2<sup>nd</sup> Battalion of the same Regiment. By coincidence, another Drinkstone resident, 2<sup>nd</sup> Lieutenant Duncan Vere Webb, was also enrolled in the 3<sup>rd</sup> Leicesters, having recently graduated from Sandhurst, and was sent for training at Fort Purbrook in early October 1914. It is quite possible that Cornish and Webb would have encountered each other at this time, though as an NCO and a commissioned officer it is unlikely that this would have been in a social context.

James Cornish boarded a ship at Southampton on 11<sup>th</sup> December, disembarking in France the following day, and was ordered to join the 2<sup>nd</sup> Battalion which was already there. At the outbreak of the War, the 2<sup>nd</sup> Battalion had been stationed in Ranikhet, India, but it was hurriedly recalled and went to France as the British Battalion of the Garhwal Brigade of the 7<sup>th</sup> (Meerut) Indian Division. It fought on the Western Front from October 1914 until November 1915.

At the beginning of March 1915, the Meerut Division, including the 2<sup>nd</sup> Leicesters, lined up before the village of Neuve Chapelle, which was held by German forces, halfway between Bethune and Lille, south of Armentières in the Artois region of northern France.

*British soldiers hold a trench in front of Neuve Chapelle 1915*

The plan was to form up overnight 9th/10th March. The 2nd Leicesters were in position by 5.00 am. A sustained artillery bombardment of the German lines was due to start at 7.30 am to discourage resistance and to cut the enemy's wire. As soon as the barrage was lifted, the advance would begin.

The 2nd Battalion of the Leicesters gave a good account of themselves and remained in the line, in the thick of the battle, until 13th March when it was relieved. There are no specific reports of the part played in the action by James Cornish.

Sadly, at roll call on 13th March, the first possible since the battle began, his name remained unanswered. At some stage in the fighting, Sergeant Cornish had been 'killed in action, during operations in the field'. The War Office was informed of Cornish's death on 17th March and the awful news was relayed to his next of kin, his mother Mildred Catchpole, by official army form to her address "Nr Post Office, Drinkstone, Bury St Edmunds" (the area now known as 'Blacksmith's Corner').

*James Cornish's name inscribed on Le Touret Memorial*

James Cornish's body was not recovered, and he has no known grave, but his name is inscribed among the 'missing' on Le Touret Memorial, at Richebourg about 5½ kilometres from the battlefield. However, some of his personal effects were returned to his mother – after the obligatory form-filling. There were seven items in all, including photographs, correspondence and a 15-franc note (worth about 11s 10½d at that time), which were eventually returned to Drinkstone in December 1915. At the same time, James' mother Mildred also received his outstanding pay of £12 15s 2d plus a gratuity of £2.

In April 1919, the War Office sent a form to the relative named as "next of kin" of each serviceman who had died during the War. In James Cornish's case, this was Mildred Catchpole, and she was asked to complete a statement listing all close relatives, so that a special plaque and commemorative scroll could be sent in memory of her son. A counter-signature by a minister or magistrate was also required, to confirm these details ~ the Reverend FH Horne of Drinkstone Rectory duly obliged.

The form Mildred completed has survived and other family members recorded as 'next of kin' are:

| Brother | Archie Cornish | Newmarket |
| Brother | Frank Cornish | Rougham |
| Brother | George (Cornish) Catchpole | Munster Fusiliers, France |
| Half Brother | Jeffrey Charles Catchpole | Drinkstone |

Ultimately, James Cornish's service medals – 1914 Star, British War Medal, Victory Medal, were also sent to Mildred Catchpole. In addition, on 27th September 1919, a War Gratuity of £8 was authorised to be paid to Mildred, James' 'sole legatee'.

There is no actual evidence to prove that James Cornish lived in Drinkstone, but his mother and brothers did. So his name appears on the framed 'Roll of Honour' (for those who were serving King and Country in 1914/15) and the memorial plaque, both in All Saints' Church. His name also appears on the war memorial in Rougham churchyard, a parish in which he was born, lived and worked. James Cornish is still remembered in Drinkstone more than a century after his death – the first of eighteen Drinkstone men, whose names are inscribed on the village war memorials, to die as a result of service in the World Wars.

*James Cornish's name on the Rougham War Memorial*

*No photographs of Harry Seeley have yet been found.*
*This is a Suffolk Regiment Private from the Great War period.*

# HARRY SEELEY

Private, 2nd Battalion Suffolk Regiment
Army Number 6620
*KILLED IN ACTION 16th June 1915*

Harry Seeley was born in Norton, Suffolk on 8th March 1876, the eldest of eight children of Elijah James (a carpenter) and Fanny (née Crick) Seeley.

According to the 1881 census, the Seeley family was living in Woolpit Road, Norton. By the next census in 1891, Harry (aged 15) was already working on the land as an agricultural labourer and living with his parents and five siblings in Doctors Lane, Norton. He was still in Norton in 1901, the year of the next census, but now in Tostock Road, with his widowed mother and four younger brothers; his occupation (and incidentally that of his two siblings, Frank, aged 16 and Chas, aged 13) is given as 'poulter's labourer' (a poulter looks after, sells or prepares poultry). By the time of the 1911 census, the family are still in Tostock Road and the four sons, who continue to live at home, are described as 'farm labourers'.

Living as a farm labourer in the early 20th century was not easy. Some looked for relief from everyday drudgery, insufficient food, low and inconsistent wages and other hardships by joining the forces - and this is precisely what Harry Seeley did. In mid-October 1903 he joined the Suffolk Regiment. At this time soldiers usually served for 6/7 years, and then for a further 5 years in the Reserve. Back in 'civvy street', during the closing months of 1912 Harry married widow Mary Ann Horrex (née Game), from Norton. The newly married couple and the children from Mary Ann's first marriage, May Horrex (aged 11) and Albert Horrex (aged 2), moved to Drinkstone, probably to Garden House (a large house divided into tenements), off the Rattlesden Road. On 28th February the following year, a daughter, Bessie Agnes, was born to the couple.

When war was declared on 4th August 1914, Seeley received his summons to 'return to the colours' and report to the Suffolk Regiment depot in Bury St Edmunds. As soon as 15th August, he was landing with the 2nd Battalion at Le Havre, France, and hurrying off by long troop train to confront the Germans outside Mons in Belgium.

Although not mentioned by name in the official accounts, Private Seeley had his first taste of action with the 2nd Suffolks on 23rd August, defending the line of the Mons-Conde Canal. The Germans advanced rapidly, backed by massed artillery, and British forces were obliged to carry out an orderly retreat.

By 4.00 am on 26th August, the 2nd Suffolks had reached the Cambrai-Le Cateau road and were told "You are going to fight it out here". The Suffolks took up a line in a stubble field on which some corn stooks were still standing. An official account states *The Suffolks in particular, who lay to the west of Le Cateau, were badly placed for general action*". In the subsequent battle of Le Cateau, which features on the regimental colours, the 2nd Battalion carried out a rear-guard defence, out-manned and out-gunned by superior numbers. After more than eight hours of incessant bombardment and fighting, with German planes circling overhead and dropping smoke bombs of different colours to direct their artillery, the Battalion was almost entirely decimated - but would not surrender. Its members were eventually overwhelmed and those that could escape did, but most were either killed or taken prisoner. At roll call the following day the War Diary noted who was left: *"Officers*

*(Captain Blackwell and Lieutenant Oates), 1 Medical Officer (Captain Phelan R.A.M.C.), A Coy - 31, B - 19, C - 38, D - 16, Attached - 7. Total 114"* (out of almost 1000 men). Battalion losses in killed, wounded or captured, were a staggering 88%.*

Among survivors, but probably not included in the above figures, was Harry Seeley - but he had been wounded, badly enough to be sent back home to England. Under the heading *'Admissions of wounded non-commissioned officers and men from the Expeditionary Force to the Royal Victoria Hospital, Netley, reported under date August 29th'* in the weekly illustrated newspaper 'The Graphic', was included *'Seeley, 620 Pte. H., Suffolk R.'* (a slight misprint here: Seeley's Army No. was actually 6620).

It is unclear how long Harry was in hospital, recovering from his wounds. A period of recovery and regrouping for the remnants of the 2nd Suffolks followed, before duties back in the trenches resumed in the winter, with more action around Kemmel (about six miles south west of Ypres) in December. Christmas day 1914 was spent in billets in the Belgian village of Westoutre. In general, the Battalion took part in 'various winter operations'.

At the beginning of June 1915, the 2nd Battalion was kept busy digging trenches around Brielen and Ouderdom, near Ypres. This was carried out under the cover of darkness as it was safer but, nonetheless, several men were wounded. By the 6th, the 2nd Suffolks were in bivouacs at Brandhoek, followed by a week in the trenches at Hooge.

*\* The 'Retreat from Mons' and the fight-to-the-last-man defence at Le Cateau were, in fact, successes in tactical terms, slowing the enemy advance and buying time to save Paris from being overwhelmed by German forces.*

*Suffolk Regiment soldiers at the notorious Hill 60, south of Ypres, 1915*

*2nd Battalion men digging trenches after the Battle of Bellewaarde, 26 May 1915*

At 4.15am on Wednesday 16th June to the west of Ypres, an attack was launched by British 3rd Division forces on German positions in front of Railway Wood and beyond it, Y Wood. This attack, on Bellewaarde, is sometimes referred to as 'The Battle of Hooge or Menin Road' and was fought in an area between the Menin Road and the Ypres-Roulers railway line. Behind an artillery 'creeping barrage', B and D Companies successfully reached Y Wood without casualties and, indeed, progressed through it. However, due to a miscalculation of timing, coupled with a slowing of the advance on either side of the Wood, the allied bombardment was inflicting casualties on its own troops.

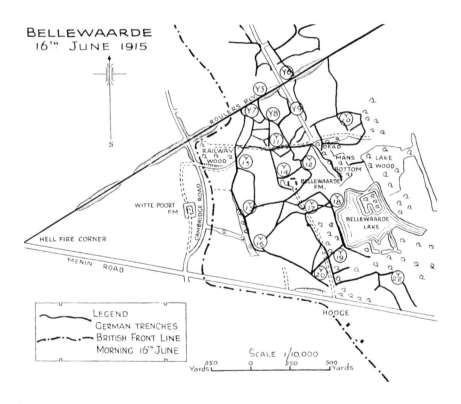

The official Battalion War Diary takes up the story:

*"Our own artillery shelled our men heavily as it had been calculated that it would take some time to get through .... (at) about 10.00am portions of the KSLI* [King's Shropshire Light Infantry] *and KRR's* [King's Royal Rifle Corps] *began to arrive .... They were supposed to do a fresh attack through our line. They none of them knew where they were and were scattered ... all the way back to Ypres. This was in no way their fault, as practically no guides had been provided ... consequently the Battalions did not get up to the firing line till about 2.00pm, with the help of all our orderlies, servants, etc to show them the way, and suffered immense and unnecessary casualties through exposing themselves to artillery in known bad spots".*

16 men were wounded and five killed, including Pte H Seeley, 6620, "killed by artillary" *[sic]*. His body was not recovered, and he has no known grave, but his name is inscribed on the Memorial of the Missing at the Menin Gate in Ypres.

*2nd Battalion War diary entry recording Private Seeley's death*

The fateful message reporting Harry Seeley's death would have been delivered to his wife Mary Ann, Kate, Albert and young Bessie back at Garden House in Rattlesden Road, Drinkstone and relayed to his mother Fanny at Heath Road, Norton. The Bury Free Press (BFP) carried the following sombre announcement a few weeks later, on page two of the 10th July 1915 edition:

*"The following sorrowful records are from the latest casualty lists: -*

*We regret to announce the death in action in France of Private Harry Seeley 2nd Battalion Suffolk Regiment. Deceased soldier was much respected in Drinkstone and the deepest sympathy is extended to the bereaved window [sic] in her loss."*

It was not until January 1916 that Harry Seeley's outstanding pay - £7 11s. 11d. (£7.59½) was forwarded to his widow Mary Ann. She received a further £5 as a War Gratuity in June 1919. By this time, Bessie had already enrolled (in 1918) as a pupil at Drinkstone School. The family address at this time is recorded as being 'Shop Corner, Drinkstone' by the Commonwealth War Graves Commission.

Harry Seeley's service medals - 1914 Star, British War Medal, Victory Medal - as well as the Memorial Plaque would have been sent to Mary Ann Seeley. A clasp for the Star (together with two small silver roses) was instituted in 1919, awarded to those who had served under fire in France or Belgium between 5 August and 22 November 1914. The clasp had to be claimed personally by the recipients, of whom a large number had either died before 1919, so it is possible that Seeley's clasp was never issued.

*Menin Gate, Ypres*

| | |
|---|---|
| LANGLEY S. L. | SAVAGE W. |
| LAY O. | SCARFE M. |
| LAYTON A. | SCARR R. |
| LAZELL W. J. | SCHOFIELD F. |
| LEACH W. | SCOTT T. W. |
| LEE B. | SCOTT W. H. |
| LEECH J. E. | SEATON E. F. |
| LEWIS P. | SEELEY H. |
| LINSKEY E. | SENTANCE J. |
| LOWE J. | SEVERN A. |
| LUCAS W. C. | SHARMAN H. |
| McCARTHY T. J. | SHARMAN W. H. |
| MACKENDER E. | SHEAD H. E. |
| MAIDWELL H. | SHEPHERD A. D. |
| MALYON A. | SHEPPARD I. |

*Harry Seeley's name inscribed on the Menin Gate in Ypres*

As well as having his name inscribed on the war memorial plaque in All Saints', it also appears on the 'Roll of Honour' (compiled during 1915) in the Church - though not quite: he is listed as 'Henry'.

*Family Notes*

Harry Seeley's widow Mary Ann married a third time, to Will Taylor. The daughter from her first marriage (to Alfred Horrex), May Kate Horrex, later married Jim Bloomfield; they had 8 children including Percy Bloomfield (who died during the Second World War and whose story is told later in this book) and David Bloomfield, who recalled his 'Granny Taylor' in Sheila Wright's book 'Drinkstone Revisited' (2007):

*"Granny Taylor used to go round the village [Drinkstone] on her bike looking after people, and she was also the midwife. I used to go everywhere with [her brother] Uncle Albert [Horrex]. We would travel to Bury to Auntie Bessie's, who was his half-sister [Harry and Mary Ann Seeley's daughter], to tend her garden".*

22

Harry and Mary Ann's daughter, Bessie married Bert Smith and they had a daughter, Josephine in 1936. The family lived in Bury St Edmunds, where Bessie died in 1992, aged 79.

*James Gill, aged about 5*

# JAMES GILL

Private, 2nd (later 1st) Battalion Suffolk Regiment
Army Number 8716
*DIED OF WOUNDS 6th October 1915*

James Gill was born on 9th November 1895 in Bury St Edmunds, eldest of seven children of James and Agnes (née Sheppard) Gill. James Gill senior was a career soldier of more than 22 years with the Suffolk Regiment (his brother Walter, James Gill junior's uncle, also served with the Suffolks). As a consequence, James junior moved home several times in his early years.

The 1901 census places the family at 15 South Street, Ipswich. Another archive from the same year records 5-year-old James being admitted as a pupil at St Matthew's Voluntary Controlled Primary School in Ipswich on 18th March 1901, with his parent listed as James Gill, a 'sergeant'. From 11th May 1903, James junior was enrolled at St James's National School, Bury St Edmunds (though his previous school is given as Victoria Street School, Bury) and living at 11 West Street, Bury; his last recorded attendance there was 20th February 1906. James' final school was Drinkstone National/Voluntary School, with his date of admission (and that of his siblings Agnes, Albert and Victoria [Gladys]) as 7th January 1907. Moving to Drinkstone was a return 'home' for the Gills, as James Gill senior had been born in the village in 1867, as had his father and his grandfather.

At the time of the 1911 census, the Gills were living at New Cottage, The Green, Drinkstone and James junior's occupation was described as a 'Domestic Groom', aged 15. However, at the end of May 1913 when he was 17½, more or less as soon as he was able, James junior followed in his father and uncle's footsteps by joining the Suffolk Regiment (2nd Battalion). At this time soldiers usually served for 7 years initially, with an option to renew, and then for a further 5 years in the Reserve. James was serving with the Battalion at The Curragh in Ireland when Britain declared war on Germany (4th August 1914) and the call came to mobilise for war.

By 23rd August, James was landing as a member of a second contingent of the 2nd Battalion at Le Havre, France and, just like fellow Drinkstonian Harry Seeley, he was rushed off to face the invading German forces in Belgium. Private Gill is not mentioned in the official accounts, but like Private Seeley he was probably in action on 26th August, during the 'Retreat from Mons'. His experiences at this time would have mirrored those of Seeley along the Cambrai-Le Cateau road and in the subsequent battle of Le Cateau. Among survivors of that engagement was James Gill, but whether he was wounded and needed time to recover, we have no evidence as his army service papers have not survived.

At some time later Gill was transferred to the 1st Battalion of the Suffolk Regiment, although the 1st Suffolks did not serve on the Western Front until 18th January 1915. Gill's service record is unclear until the following September, when he was certainly deployed with the 1st Suffolks at the Battle of Loos and had been promoted to acting corporal. When the 1st Battalion arrived at Noyelles-les-Vermelles in the battle area on 27th September 1915, the main attack had taken place, but nevertheless the fighting was far from over.

The Suffolks were ordered to support the attack by the 1st Welch Regiment and 2nd Cheshire Regiment on the so-called 'Little Willie' trench system, part of the German Hohenzollern Redoubt. On 3rd October the Battalion was ordered to join the attack, due to begin at 8.30pm, but was *"unable to make sufficient progress owing to the crowded state of the communication trench ... the Battalion not having arrived, zero hour was postponed till 10.30, and then till midnight. Actually, the attack did not begin till nearly 2am."* By that time, the position of the moon had changed and other points of reference for the attack had altered or disappeared; there was no artillery support. Three companies of the Battalion began to grope their way forward but with direction completely lost, the attack went awry and failed. Casualties were heavy and around 160 officers and men were missing, killed or wounded. Among those wounded was acting Corporal James Gill.

*Suffolk soldiers coming out of the line c.4<sup>th</sup> Oct 1915*

Having received first aid in the trenches, Gill was passed to an advance dressing station and eventually admitted to the 10<sup>th</sup> Stationary Hospital in St Omer, some 40-odd miles from the battlefield. It was here, on Wednesday 6<sup>th</sup> October 1915, that James Gill died as a result of his wounds. He was buried in Longuenesse (St. Omer) Souvenir Cemetery, Pas de Calais, France (reference II. A. 50.).

The message reporting James Gill's death would have been delivered to his parents James and Agnes Gill, by now possibly having moved to New England, near Sible Hedingham in Essex.

But there is likely to have been someone else, apart from immediate family, who would mourn and shed tears at the news of his death. Miss Lilian (Lily) Harvey, who was just 19 years old, lived in Park Cottages at Drinkstone Park and had attended Drinkstone School from 1896. She was named as James' legatee and it was she, rather than his parents or siblings, who received his outstanding army pay of £9 5s. 10d (£9.29p) on 1st March 1916 and a War Gratuity of £7 10s. (£7.50p) on 30th August 1919. Would it be too presumptive to say that Lily was, perhaps, James' sweetheart?

After the war, James Gill's service medals (1914 Star, British War Medal, Victory Medal), Memorial Plaque and scroll would have been sent to his parents, his next of kin. As well as appearing on the war memorial, James Gill is listed on the 'Roll of Honour' which also hangs in Drinkstone's All Saints' Church.

*Family Notes*

James' father, James Gill senior, had joined up again on 31st October 1914 at the age of 48 years and 8 months, in the 3rd Battalion (Special Reserve) of the Suffolk Regiment as an acting Colour Sergeant. He was subsequently transferred to the 10th Battalion and promoted to Sergeant Major and was employed in Britain in the home Training Reserve Battalion from September 1916. He was discharged as no longer being physically fit for war service on 26th June 1917.

James' brother, Albert Edward Gill joined the Royal Navy in February 1915, serving as a Boy at HMS Ganges and progressing during the War to Able Bodied Seaman, last serving on HMS Pembroke I. He subsequently emigrated to Canada in 1923.

James' sister Gladys Victoria Gill (another pupil at Drinkstone School) married William Albert Pryke, who served during the

War in the 8th Suffolks (the younger brother of Arthur Pryke – *see later*), on 12th February 1920 at Drinkstone Parish Church. The couple had 6 children, including William Arthur Pryke (named after his father and uncle?) who died in 1942 on the SS Lisbon Maru. Gladys died on 26th August 1995 in Halstead, Essex, aged 94.

# ALBERT SMITH

1st Battalion Prince of Wales's Own (West Yorkshire Regiment)
Army Number 15241
*KILLED IN ACTION 4th March 1916*

Albert Edward Smith was born on 17th December 1896 in Felsham, the third youngest of nine children of John and Ellen (née Pilbrow) Smith, both also born in Felsham. His father was an agricultural labourer and later a horseman on a farm, and his mother was a domestic servant at Bradfield St Clare Rectory, before her marriage to John in 1883.

In the census taken in March 1901, Albert was aged 4 and living with his parents, four older siblings and 5-year-old cousin Beatrice Pilbrow, in Cockfield Road, near Quakers Farm, Felsham (about halfway to Cockfield). During 1905 the Smith family moved to Drinkstone, as both Albert and Beatrice were enrolled in that year at Drinkstone School (No's 244 & 245), having transferred from the school in Felsham.

*Felsham School early 20th Century*

By the census of April 1911, the Smith family's address was recorded as Drinkstone Green but Albert, now 14, had left school and was staying with his aunt and uncle, Susannah and Walter Osborne at Grange Farmhouse in Thorpe Morieux. His occupation was given as 'farm labourer' – possibly on Grange Farm where his uncle Walter was farm bailiff.

We have no further record of Albert Smith until September 1914 when he volunteered for the army in York, joining the Prince of Wales's Own (West Yorkshire Regiment). Why Albert was in York at this time, so far from home, is not known – maybe a search for work led him north? He probably enlisted in the early days of September when recruitment, fuelled by patriotic fervour, tales of German atrocities and alarm following the 'Retreat from Mons' was at its height. Albert was still only 17¾, the legal age for service overseas being 19 years old. Thus, training and home service followed until he was posted to France, arriving on 10th December 1915, one week shy of his 19th birthday.

He joined the 1st Battalion of the West Yorks Regiment, who were serving in and around the Belgian city of Ypres. The Regimental War Diaries for that period reveal that the next three months of Albert's service were a rather repetitive routine of duties between the trenches, the battered city and behind the lines. The official Regimental History describes it thus, *"The awful unrest of the Ypres Salient had by this time become proverbial. The Battalion spent its unenviable existence either in the front line trenches of the St. Julien Sector, along the banks of the Yser Canal, or in billets in Poperinghe"*. Typically, this meant working parties at night (where the tasks were digging out and repairing trenches, dugouts, relief lines and billets) and carrying ammunition and other supplies to the front line.

*Ypres Cloth Hall and St Martin's Cathedral, 23rd January 1916*

Although Albert Smith probably did not take part in any actual fighting at this time, he certainly experienced life 'under fire' with shelling frequent ~ *"Violent shell fire continued to characterise the whole of February"*, as well as enemy sniping and even one gas attack.

In the early hours of 1st March 1916, the 1st Battalion of the West Yorks relieved the Durham Light Infantry in the trenches for what was to be a week-long duty. The Regimental History records *"On the 2nd March, the 17th Division attacked The Bluff .... In this attack the 6th Division* [of which the 1st West Yorks were a part] *co-operated ... (with) the West Yorkshiremen .... opening rapid fire while the attack was proceeding"*. The Regimental War Diary takes up the story for Saturday 4th March:

*"Trenches. Snow fell all morning after a wet night, enemy very quiet during night, 'S' Line shelled in afternoon .... Casualties: 1 killed – 4 wounded."*

The soldier killed was evidently Private Albert Smith, aged 19. Reports in the BFP of the 1st and 8th July refer to 'A gallant young Drinkstone soldier' of the 1st Batt West Yorks Regiment, 6th Platoon, killed in action by a shell. He was buried in the Potijze Burial Ground Cemetery (plot G.2), a little more than a mile from the Menin Gate in Ypres. Albert's death was all the more poignant since the Battalion left the trenches just over a week later, and the following 5 weeks were spent well away from the Front, resting and training in camp near Calais.

The sad news of Albert's death was delivered to his parents John and Ellen back in Drinkstone. His service medals - 1914-15 Star, British War Medal and Victory Medal - as well as the

Memorial Plaque and scroll would have been sent to his family. As registered next-of-kin, his father John received his outstanding army pay of £5 16s. 1d (£5.80½p) on 9th June 1916 and a War Gratuity of £6 on 16th August 1919. Albert Smith's name is inscribed on the war memorial and on the 'Roll of Honour' (compiled during 1915) in Drinkstone's All Saints' Church; his name also appears on a memorial plaque in Felsham School (now the Village Hall) in memory of former pupils. Curiously, although he and both his parents were born in Felsham, his name was not included on that village's war memorial in St Peter's Church.

*Memorial plaque to former pupils of Felsham School*

*No photographs of Thomas Barker have yet been found. This is Private Thomas Sharman, also of the 7th Battalion, Suffolk Regiment, from Lowestoft. He was killed in action on 3rd July 1916 at the Battle for Ovillers, aged 27, the same action in which Thomas Barker sustained his fatal wounds.*

# THOMAS BARKER

7th Battalion Suffolk Regiment
Army Number 23621
*DIED OF WOUNDS 4th July 1916*

Thomas James Barker was born in Bradfield St George, Suffolk on 12th August 1883 and baptised in the village on 16th September of that year. He was the second son of six children born to Ebenezer Barker, a farm labourer, and his wife Roseann (née Pettit), only three of whom were still living at the time the 1911 census was taken.

In the census of April 1891, the Barker family was living in Felsham Road, Bradfield St George. At the time of the next census, in March 1901, they were in Mill Road in the same village and Thomas' occupation was given as 'farm labourer'. By April 1911, the Barkers were living in a two-up, two-down cottage in the Gedding Road, Drinkstone and Thomas was described as a 'labourer on a farm' but having 'no work'. It is not clear when the Barkers moved to Drinkstone, but a Wilfred Barker was enrolled at Drinkstone School in 1908 – the same name as Thomas' youngest sibling, listed in the 1911 census as a 'scholar' and aged 11 – which probably gives a clue to when the Barkers might have arrived in the village.

There is one other, rather intriguing, item that appears to refer to Thomas Barker at about this time. The BFP of 16th September 1911 carries an advertisement in its 'classified' section which reads *"For Sale, Disc Phonograph, with 11 double side and 11 single records, in good going order, £2 5s.\* – Apply T. Barker, Felsham Road, Drinkstone, Bury St. Edmunds"*.     * = £2.25p

39

This 'ad' appeared fewer than 6 months after the 1911 census (when only one family by the name of Barker was listed as living in Drinkstone). Agricultural workers at the time probably earned no more than 15s. (.75p) per week (if, indeed, work could be found); gramophone records probably cost between 3s. (15p) and 5s. (25p) each in the shops, so, if this is the same 'T.Barker', it is surprising to find a farm labourer apparently owning (let alone selling) a gramophone and records for the equivalent of three weeks wages.

Thomas Barker's service records have not survived, but from calculations based on other records relating to his Army Number, it would appear that he enlisted as a volunteer* in the 7th Battalion of the Suffolk Regiment in Bury St Edmunds, aged 32, in mid-December 1915. Training in Britain would have followed, until Private Barker was posted to France at some time in the spring/early summer 1916.

*Conscription did not begin until 2nd March 1916*

The Regimental War Diary for May 1916 records that on the 9th and 14th of that month, 58 and 68 'other ranks' respectively joined for duty with the Battalion. It is quite likely that Thomas was included among these drafts.

For the next few weeks, the Battalion occupied itself with resting, training and preparation. In mid-June the Battalion moved by train to Vignacourt, near Amiens, in the Somme region. Tellingly, for eight consecutive days the men practised assaulting trenches and attacks on 'further positions': the 'Big Push' – the Battle of the Somme – was about to begin. The Battalion moved eastwards and on 2nd July it took over support trenches near Albert. It was here that the Suffolks received orders to make an attack the following day at 3.15 am, on the village of Ovillers held by the Germans, over a frontage of 200 yards. Ten minutes before zero hour, the leading waves advanced under cover of bombardment. The Regimental History recorded what happened next.

*"The Battalion assaulted in eight successive waves ... The first four waves penetrated as far as the enemy's third line, portions of them getting into the village itself; but owing to the darkness the succeeding waves lost touch, enabling the Germans to surge in and cut them off. At the third line of resistance, after very heavy fighting the assault was brought to a standstill [at about 4.30pm], the Battalion losing very heavily".*

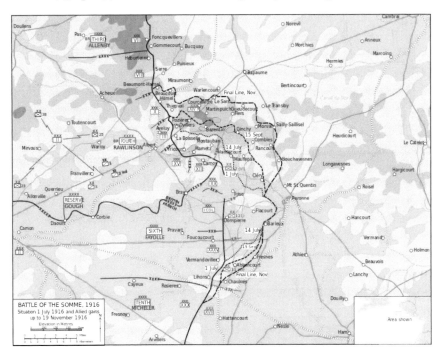

Many men lay out in no man's land, waiting to be saved – many dying from wounds which could have been easily treated had they been able to return to their own lines. The medical services were swamped in the early days of the Somme by the sheer volume of casualties, for which they were not prepared.

*Men of the Cheshire Regiment occupy a captured German trench at Ovillers*

Casualties in the Battalion were 21 officers and 458 other ranks killed, wounded and missing. One of these casualties was evidently Private Thomas Barker, badly wounded.

*Cap badge found on the battlefield at Ovillers, where the 7th Suffolks made their attack on 3rd July 1916. It was discovered a few years ago by a First World War enthusiast lying on the surface about 10 yards from the cemetery wall.*

Somehow Private Barker was brought back to British lines. After receiving initial first aid he would have been taken to an advance dressing station close to the front line manned by men of the 36th Field Ambulance, Royal Army Medical Corps. Sad to say, Thomas Barker died from his wounds on 4th July aged 33, fewer than two months since he had first landed in France. He was buried in the Millencourt Communal Cemetery Extension (plot A.20), about 6 miles from the battlefield where he was wounded. Surprisingly, Thomas' gravestone was inscribed with the wrong year of death – 1917 instead of 1916! This seems to have been due, literally, to a typing error at the Commonwealth War Graves Commission. In the middle of a long list of names and details about burials at Millencourt Cemetery, relating to soldiers who died in early July 1916, is Thomas Barker's name with a date of death given as 4th July 1917.

*Courtesy: britishwargraves.co.uk*

43

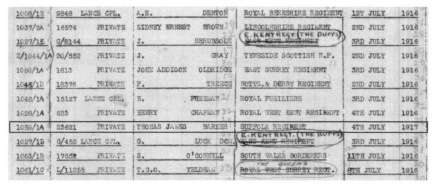

| | | | | | | | | |
|---|---|---|---|---|---|---|---|---|
| 1008/1E | 9848 | LANCE CPL. | A.E. | DENTON | ROYAL BERKSHIRE REGIMENT | 1ST JULY | 1916 |
| 1037/2A | 16574 | PRIVATE | SIDNEY ERNEST | BROWN | LINCOLNSHIRE REGIMENT / E. KENT REGT. (THE BUFFS) | 2ND JULY | 1916 |
| 1027/1E | G/8144 | PRIVATE | J. | SHRUBSOLE | EAST KENT REGIMENT | 3RD JULY | 1916 |
| 2/1044/1A | 20/552 | PRIVATE | J. | GRAY | TYNESIDE SCOTTISH N.F. | 2ND JULY | 1916 |
| 1060/1A | 1813 | PRIVATE | JOHN ADDISON | OLDRIDGE | EAST SURREY REGIMENT | 3RD JULY | 1916 |
| 1045/1D | 18376 | PRIVATE | F. | TREECE | NOTTS. & DERBY REGIMENT | 2ND JULY | 1916 |
| 1048/1A | 15127 | LANCE CPL. | H. | FREEMAN | ROYAL FUSILIERS | 3RD JULY | 1916 |
| 1028/1A | 823 | PRIVATE | HENRY | CHAPMAN | ROYAL WEST KENT REGIMENT | 4TH JULY | 1916 |
| 1059/1A | 23621 | PRIVATE | THOMAS JAMES | BARKER | SUFFOLK REGIMENT | 4TH JULY | 1917 |
| 1027/1B | G/452 | LANCE CPL. | G. | LUCK DCM. | E. KENT REGT. (THE BUFFS) EAST KENT REGIMENT | 3RD JULY | 1916 |
| 1063/1B | 17552 | PRIVATE | S. | O'CONNELL | SOUTH WALES BORDERERS | 11TH JULY | 1916 |
| 1061/1C | L/11255 | PRIVATE | T.G.O. | YELDHAM | THE QUEEN'S ROYAL WEST SURREY REGT. | 8TH JULY | 1916 |

*CWGC burial record for Private Barker with wrong year of death*

Ebenezer and Rose Ann, Thomas' parents, were informed of his death back at the Green in Drinkstone. Eventually, when peace came, his service medals - British War Medal, Victory Medal, along with the Memorial Plaque and scroll were despatched to his family. Thomas' outstanding army pay of £3 16s. 8d (£3.83½p) was sent to Ebenezer Barker on 9th February 1917 and a War Gratuity of £3 followed on 11th August 1919.

*War memorial in St Peter's Church, Felsham*

44

Thomas Barker's name is inscribed on the war memorial in All Saints' Church, Drinkstone. It is also the first name that appears on the war memorial in St Peter's Church, Felsham although, to date, no firm evidence has been found proving that he lived or worked in Felsham. However, there is an inference that the Barkers had lived in Felsham, at some time between 1901 and 1908: the Drinkstone School pupil enrolment register for Wilfred Barker, Thomas' youngest brother (mentioned above), reads 'Previous School: Felsham'.

*Family Notes*

Thomas' brother Wilfred (born in 1899, so 16 years his junior) was conscripted into the Army Training Reserve in October 1917 and was subsequently assigned to the Queen's Royal Regiment (West Surrey). He was gassed on 23rd August 1918 and transferred to the Labour Corps, having returned to duty at the end of September. He was demobilised in February 1919 and returned to the family home, by now situated in Chapel Road, Drinkstone. He was finally discharged from the army on 13th January 1920.

# WALTER HALLS

8th Battalion Suffolk Regiment
Army Number 22985
*DIED OF WOUNDS 28th July 1916*

Walter Ernest Halls was born in Drinkstone on 28th December 1892, probably at the family home in Rattlesden Road, the second of 10 children (of whom 9 survived) of Charles and Emily (née Holland) Halls and was named after his paternal grandfather. He was enrolled in Drinkstone National School on 9th Sept 1897 aged four and left on 5th December 1907 a few weeks short of his 15th birthday, having reached school-leaving age. He joined the family grocery business in Rattlesden Road, Drinkstone Green in premises that are now a private dwelling called 'The White House'.

*The Halls' shop, Rattlesden Road, now The White House, March 2019*
*Courtesy: Yvonne & Richard Bolt*

In the 1911 census, the family was still living at The Green, Drinkstone. The occupations of Walter (then aged 18), his elder brother Bertie (age 20) and their mother, were given as assistants in the grocery and drapery shop run by Charles Halls. The entire Halls family of 11 lived on the shop premises, the business successful enough to support the whole family, with Charles' business acumen apparently acquired when working at his own father's grocery business in Woolpit Green.

In addition to his work at the shop, Walter was a member of the Wesleyan Chapel in Gedding Road, Drinkstone and was also a Sunday School teacher. He was still working as a grocery assistant when he volunteered for the 12th Battalion of the Suffolk Regiment at Bury St Edmunds in November 1915.

The next six months were concerned with training: he was stationed in Bury to begin with, but after a few months he was sent to Colchester attached to the 10th Suffolks, and then moved to Dovercourt, Essex. He was subsequently posted to France at the end of May 1916 to join the 8th Battalion. The official War Diary records that reinforcements (49 'other ranks') joined the 8th Battalion, at Carnoy on the Somme, on 28th May 1916 and Walter Halls is likely to have been among these.

During June, elements of the 8th Battalion continued to train (at the Divisional School in Corbie) and prepare for 'the Big Push' that was to come. Some time was also spent at Grovetown Camp and in billets at Bronfay Farm and, though not in the immediate front line, it was not immune from danger. On the 3rd June, a single shell fell in the farm courtyard - the Regimental War Diary recorded the outcome: *Three drummers killed, eight wounded, three shell shock*.

Although the 8th Battalion was not one of those earmarked for the initial attack at the start of the Battle of the Somme on 1st July, its members held front-line trenches during the preliminary artillery bombardment, by far the heaviest ever witnessed. Walter and his fellows were held in reserve, but not called upon; nevertheless, they worked doggedly, carrying ammunition, water and other materials to the front.

On the 2nd July, the 8th Suffolks took over the front-line trenches, but were still not involved in any of the desperate fighting. After a rest period, the Battalion was back in the line again (on the 14th) and due to take part in an attack on Guillemont and Ginchy. This action was abandoned when German counter-attacks re-took the village of Longueval and the greater part of Delville Wood. However, at midnight on 18th/19th July, the 53rd Brigade of which the 8th Suffolks were a part, (in the words of the official Regimental History) *'was unexpectedly launched, at very short notice and without reconnaissance, in a most unenviable counter-attack, designed with the object of clearing the village and wood'.*

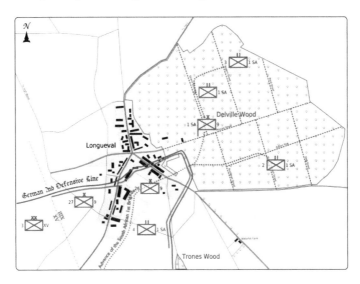

It was already dawn when the Brigade was ready and in position. Two miles of open country had to be crossed, in broad daylight, before the objective would be reached, with every available German gun aimed at the advancing troops. The Suffolks moved forward resolutely, coming under machine gun fire and encountering strong resistance, especially around Longueval church; heavy casualties were sustained.

After a day of fierce fighting, the Suffolks consolidated their position. Although the attack did not achieve its main objectives, the line in the village had advanced about 300 yards and the dangerous bottle neck entrance to Delville Wood was considerably widened, greatly facilitating safer access for the allied troops occupying the Wood. However, Battalion casualties had been considerable: from the 18th to the morning of the 21st July, eight officers and 235 other ranks had been killed, wounded and missing. It would appear that among these was Private Walter Halls. In a printed record of the 8th Battalion (1915-1918) published after the War, Private Walter Halls is recorded as having died at Delville Wood on 18th July 1916, but this is most probably incorrect; it is more likely that it was on the 19th July that he was wounded in the attack on Longueval/Delville Wood.

After administering initial first aid, the medical services removed Walter Halls to an advance dressing station near the front line. His wounds were considered serious enough for him to be moved by hospital train to the 18th General Hospital at Camiers, about 16 miles south of Boulogne. Sadly, Walter did not recover and died from his wounds on 28th July 1916 aged 23, fewer than two months after he had first landed in France. He was buried in Étaples Military Cemetery (plot IX. A. 8A.), about 4 miles south of the hospital in which he died.

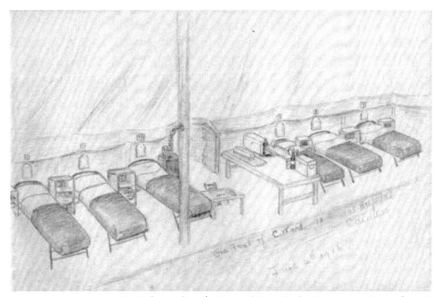

*Tented ward, 18th General Hospital, Camiers ~ June 4th 1916*
*Sketch by VAD Nurse Evelyn Jackson*

The news of Walter's death was delivered to his parents Charles, Emily and the rest of his family back in Rattlesden Road, Drinkstone. Sister M Davis (Queen Alexandra's Imperial Military Nursing Service), the nurse who had attended to Walter in his last hours, kindly wrote a letter to his mother giving brief details of the circumstances of his death, which was published in the BFP of 12th August. She wrote,

*"I regret to say your boy died last night at 1a.m., poor lad... It will be a great sorrow to you. He had a hard fight for it, but went very quickly at the last. He was too ill to talk so I am afraid he was able to leave no message for you. I wish I had more to tell you and I wish it had been better news. He will be buried in a little cemetery at Étaples, four miles from here. It is beautifully kept and so pretty now with flowers on the graves. It would comfort you to see it. With much sympathy for you in*

*your great sorrow. I am sure you have lost a good son. He has done his duty. Yours sincerely, M Davis, Sister."*

The newspaper also reported *'He was beloved by a large circle of friends, being of a cheerful disposition'.*

A memorial service was held at Drinkstone Chapel on Sunday 6th August, conducted by circuit minister the Reverend George Harbottle, who *'commented on the many good qualities that marked the deceased'.*

Walter's service medals - British War Medal and Victory Medal – along with the Memorial Plaque and scroll would have been sent to his family. Designated as 'sole legatee', his mother Emily received his outstanding army pay of £3 16s. 7d (£3.83p) on 21st March 1917 and a War Gratuity of £3 on 15th October 1919.

*Family Notes*

Walter's father, Charles Louis Halls, ran the grocery business in Rattlesden Road from at least 1891 (when he was 24) until he died on 9th June 1944, aged 79. Walter's older brother, Bertie took over the shop until it closed in the 1960's. Bertie died on 12th July 1965 and is buried in the churchyard at All Saints', Drinkstone.

Bertie himself had signed up for the army in Bury St Edmunds on 2nd February 1916 and was posted to the Bedfordshire Regiment on 25th July 1916. However, he was discharged from service on 2nd September as 'not being likely to become an efficient soldier'. On 11th June 1917 he was obliged to write to the War Office to request a Silver War Badge. These had been issued from September 1916, since numbers of men discharged from the services as unfit for war service found themselves being harassed, when some women (and others) confronted men of fighting age in public places who were not in military uniform, by ostentatiously presenting them with white feathers, as a suggestion of cowardice. The badge was a means of discouraging such incidents.

# JOHN WHITING

'A' Company, 8th Battalion Suffolk Regiment
Army Number 13942
*DIED OF WOUNDS 7th August 1916*

(Samuel) John Whiting was born in Hessett on 29th December 1894, the first son of Emily Whiting, and was named after his maternal grandfather and great grandfather, both Samuel Whiting. No record has currently been found of his father's name or for any marriage for Emily. In the 1901 census, Emily and Samuel (by now called by his middle name John) were recorded as living with Emily's mother Eliza (née Bullett) and stepfather Elijah Catchpole at the Old House in Hessett.

In May 1904, a second son named Ernest E Whiting was born to Emily. He was enrolled at the Drinkstone National School in 1909, which is possibly when the family moved to Drinkstone to live in part of the house now known as The Blacksmith's Cottage in the Street.

*The Blacksmith's Cottage, August 2017*

Certainly, in the 1911 census this is where the family were living, with John Whiting's occupation given as 'under gardener' and his age as 16. According to a report in the BFP of August 19th 1916, he was employed, presumably as a gardener, by Mr Thomas Harrison-Topham at Hessett House (where his aunt Anna Whiting also worked as a live-in cook). It says that he worked here for 9 years until enlisting in the army which, if so, means he began working at the House when aged 10!

The same newspaper article reported that John Whiting had enlisted in the army (the 8th Battalion of the Suffolk Regiment) 'at the outbreak of the War', with other sources suggesting that this would have been on 2nd September 1914 (when a recruitment meeting took place at Drinkstone School). John was sent to Shorncliffe Camp, Kent for his initial training, before being posted to Colchester in early October. After a strenuous period of winter instruction, the Battalion moved to Salisbury Plain, followed by further intensive preparation at Codford, just south of the Plain.

Private Whiting was finally sent on active duty with the rest of the 8th Battalion, landing in France on 25th July 1915. After a week's rest, the Battalion received instruction in trench warfare before taking over trenches near Bray-sur-Somme and then further north near Albert, where the Suffolks received their 'initiation' in warfare as members of the 53rd Brigade. In a history of the Battalion published after the War, the next period of service was described as 'a typical trench-warfare winter', a fairly uneventful time in a quieter section of the line, which stretched into the spring. In early May 1916, training increased again with rumours of 'the Big Push' to come – the Battle of the Somme was about to begin.

The experiences of John Whiting during this period, as a member of the 8th Battalion of the Suffolks, was similar to that of Walter Halls (*see previously*), who had joined the 8th Suffolks in France at the end of May 1916. On 21st June, they moved forward to hold front-line trenches on the Somme during the preliminary artillery bombardment. At this time, on 24th June, a party from the Battalion took part in a night-time raid on the German trench, with three declared purposes: '*1. To capture prisoners. 2. To ascertain strength of enemy's front and support trenches. 3. To kill Boches and destroy his morale*'. When the big attack began, on 1st July, John Whiting and his fellows were waiting in reserve, but not called upon; nevertheless, they worked very hard, conveying ammunition, water and other provisions to the front.

As a member of the same 8th Battalion group as Walter Halls, John Whiting's record of movement, experience and life under fire during July 1916 was much the same as Walter's. John, too, endured the might of German artillery, rifle and machine gun fire in the Longueval and Delville Wood area.

The 8th Suffolks War Diary for 20th July 1916 records that *"during the afternoon, a detachment of South African troops were relieved in an advanced trench in Delville Wood. This relief was completed by 6.30pm. 'A' Company taking over"*. Private John Whiting was a member of 'A' Company and it appears that during this operation he was wounded. In the BFP item of 19th August mentioned above, it was reported that Private Whiting received a wound (later confirmed as a gunshot) on the 20th July.

After receiving initial first aid, John Whiting would have been taken to an advance dressing station near the front line. His wounds were considered serious enough for him to be moved by hospital train back to the coast, but fit enough to be evacuated back to England and the Fulham Military Hospital in London. Sadly, John Whiting finally succumbed to his wounds and died on 7th August 1916, aged 21.

*Fulham Military Hospital*

Of the fifteen men named on the Drinkstone First World War memorial, Whiting was the only one to die 'back home'. A death certificate was therefore issued, which was not the case when death occurred overseas. This provides more details relating to his death than are generally available with other casualties. The certificate was issued on 10th August, with the death being reported by Nancy G Dalziel who was present at his passing – presumably a nurse attending him during his final hours. The death was certified by WJ Hill (a doctor at the hospital?) and, following a post-mortem, the cause of death was given as:

*1. gunshot wound to the thorax   2. septic infection 3. heart failure.*

News of John's death was given to his mother Emily and the rest of his family, back in The Street, Drinkstone; this time the War Office standard 'Army Form B104-82' had but a short distance to travel – from the Post Office next door.

The BFP report described what happened next, *'Deceased was brought home and interred at Hessett, being a native of that village. Deceased mortal remains were borne to the grave by Mr J Bauly (Suffolk Yeomanry), Mr H Woodard, Mr D Bullett and Mr E Catchpole (members of the VTC\*). The relatives of the deceased desire to thank those who so kindly lined the grave with flowers and also those who sent floral tributes from Drinkstone and Hessett'.*

*\* VTC = Volunteer Training Corps (equivalent to Home Guard in the Second World War)*

The report concludes with a touching tribute, *'He was greatly respected by all who knew him. Being of a loving disposition he made many friends who sincerely mourn his loss'.*

A Commonwealth War Graves Commission headstone bearing his name stands in the churchyard of St Ethelbert in Hessett, but states that he is 'buried elsewhere in this churchyard'. Parish burial records show he was interred on 11th August, possibly in a family plot. As well as having his name etched on the Drinkstone War Memorial, John Whiting is listed on the Drinkstone Roll of Honour and among the fallen on the Hessett War Memorial, also in the churchyard.

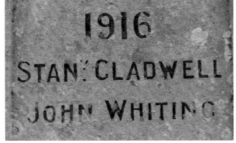

John's service medals – 1914-15 Star, British War Medal, Victory Medal - as well as the Memorial Plaque and scroll were sent to his mother, Emily. She also received his outstanding army pay of £7 8s. 6d. (£7.42½p) on 18th May 1917 and a War Gratuity of £9 on 4th July 1919.

*Family Notes*

John Whiting's mother Emily was born in Hessett in 1866, the daughter of Eliza and Samuel Whiting (who was 67 years old when she was born). Her mother subsequently remarried twice. Both Emily and her elder sister Anna (born c.1858) worked as domestic servants and both were employed as cooks. In the 1881 census, Emily was living at Newports Lane, Hessett and described as a servant; Anna was employed as a cook in Brook Green, Fulham, ironically no more than a mile from Fulham Military Hospital where her nephew John's life ended 35 years later. In 1891, both Emily and Anna were working as servants in houses in the Bath area of Somerset, just 2 miles apart from each other. In 1901, Anna was still at the same house in Bath, now described as cook, while Emily was in Hessett, looking after her 6-year-old son John. In 1911, Anna was back in Suffolk, the cook at Hessett House, and Emily was in Drinkstone with her two sons. Anna died in 1934 and was buried in All Saints' churchyard, Drinkstone – though her name is inscribed on the gravestone as 'Annie'. Emily continued to live in Drinkstone in the same house, up to 1939 at least, until her death on 9th March 1943, aged 77. She too was buried in All Saints' churchyard, sharing a plot and gravestone with her sister Anna – still close, even in death.

# SIDNEY ROSE

8th Battalion Suffolk Regiment
Army Number 14005
*KILLED IN ACTION 29th October 1916*

Sidney Arthur Rose was born in Drinkstone, Suffolk on 15th March 1887, the youngest son of the 14 children born to agricultural labourer William Rose and his wife Kezia(h) (née Butcher, formerly Last). He was baptised at All Saints' Church in Drinkstone by the Rector, Frederick Horne, on 5th June 1887.

In the 1891 census, 'Sydney' (*sic*) was living in Rattlesden Road (towards the Rattlesden end, near the White Horse beer house) and listed as a 'scholar'. Records for Drinkstone National School reveal that he was enrolled as a pupil at some time between 1885 and 1893, probably in 1891. By the next census in 1901, Sidney was 14 and had left school, his occupation given as 'ordinary agricultural labourer' and he was living with the Rose family (numbering nine in all) at The Green, Drinkstone. In 1911, Sidney was still at home with his parents, brother Cecil and two sisters; father and both boys being described as 'labourers on farm'. Sidney worked for Mr John Jewers (farmer) of Whitefield House, Drinkstone.

After War was declared in August 1914, and in the wake of the heroic 'Retreat from Mons' by the British Expeditionary Force in the early weeks, an appeal for 100,000 volunteers was launched. There was an overwhelming response. Among those eager to join up was Sidney Rose and his older brothers Cecil, Leonard (known as George) and Walter.

The East Anglian Daily Times of Friday 4th September 1914 *(see page 4)* reported that at a meeting held in Drinkstone School on the evening of Wednesday 2nd, *"fourteen recruits volunteered for enlistment, thirteen of whom were accepted"*. Indeed, Suffolk Regiment records indicate that George joined on 2nd September (Army Number 13926), on the same day and in the same Battalion as fellow villager John Whiting (Army Number 13942), who was to die of wounds on 7th August 1916; Sidney and Cecil also signed up together that same day, (Army Numbers 14005 & 14006); Walter enlisted in the 8th Suffolks too, probably later that month (Army Number 14776). An article about the Rose brothers in the BFP of 17th November 1917 says, *"After finishing their harvest, they joined up in the 8th Battn, Suffolk Regiment in September 1914"*.

Like John Whiting (*see previously*) Sidney went to Shorncliffe Camp in Kent for his initial training, then to Colchester in October. While stationed there, he married 29-year-old Eva Ann Warren of Norton (who had been working as a parlour maid at Gedding Hall at the time of the 1911 census), on 26th April 1915. Sidney's brother Cecil and Eva's sister Alice acted as witnesses. Shortly afterwards, the Battalion moved to Salisbury Plain, then on to Codford, just south of the Plain for training.

Private Sidney Rose landed on active service in France with the 8th Battalion on 25th July 1915, in the company of his three brothers and John Whiting. Sidney's experience and day-to-day routines broadly mirrored those of Whiting: time passed without particular incident in a quieter section of the line, which extended into the following spring. Meanwhile, it appears that Sidney enjoyed some home leave, but it was after he had returned to France that he received the happy news that Eva had given birth to a son, Arthur G. Rose, around March/April 1916. With intimations that 'the Big Push' was about to begin, training increased. The Battle of the Somme was imminent.

We do not have details of Sidney's role or experiences during the Battle, and although the 8th Suffolks were not part of the initial fighting from 1st July, he almost certainly took part in the attacks on Longueville and Delville Wood later in July. Having survived these actions, a period of prolonged training followed before the 8th Suffolks moved back into trenches. On 26th September, with the 10th Essex Battalion, they attacked the redoubtable fortress of Thiepval. It was swiftly overrun with the entire garrison being killed or captured, with small British losses - a substantial accomplishment. After a fortnight's rest, the Battalion returned to the trenches west of Courcellette near Albert, taking turns of duty in the lines for the next two weeks.

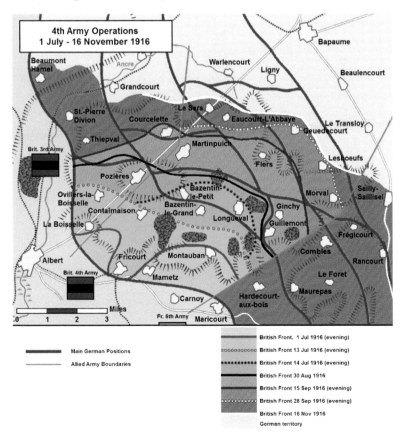

The Battalion War Diary for 29th October records *"Battalion relieved 6th Battn Northampton Regmt ... During the evening Vancouver Trench was heavily shelled:- 'A' Company ... had their Company Headquarters blown in and 5 men killed"*.

The five men were: L Cpl C Gilbey and Ptes J Fletcher, E Fenbow, S Rose and A Tweed. Private Sidney Rose has no known grave, but his name is inscribed on the Thiepval Memorial to the Missing *(Pier 1C, Face 2A)*. The BFP article of November 1917 *(mentioned above)* included part of the text of a letter from a comrade: *"Poor old Sid Rose was killed instantly. He was digging some poor fellows out who had got buried by a shell and another came and killed him, so he died doing his duty, and he couldn't do any more"*.

*Sidney Rose's name on the Thiepval Monument to the Missing*

The heart-breaking message reporting Sidney's death would have been delivered to his wife Eva and young Arthur, whom sadly Sidney never saw, and relayed to his mother and father in Rattlesden Road. On 5th March 1917, Private Rose's outstanding pay - £5 2s. 2d. (£5.11) was forwarded to his widow. She received a further £9 as a War Gratuity in August 1919.

Eventually, Sidney Rose's service medals – 1914-15 Star, British War Medal, Victory Medal - Memorial Plaque and scroll would have been sent to his widow Eva. Unhappily, Sidney and Eva's son Arthur died in 1922, aged six. Eva re-married that same year and went on to have two daughters. She died in the Norwich area in 1975.

Sidney Rose is recorded on Drinkstone's First World War Memorial. His name also appears on the framed 'Roll of Honour' (for those who were serving King and Country in 1914/15) in All Saints' Church.

# CECIL ROSE

8th Battalion Suffolk Regiment
Army Number 14006
*DIED 7th May 1917*

Cecil Robert Rose was born in Drinkstone, Suffolk on 16th February 1885, one of 14 children of agricultural labourer William Rose and his wife Kezia(h). He was baptised at All Saints', Drinkstone by the Reverend Frederick Horne on 12th April 1885.

In the 1891 census, Cecil was listed as a 'scholar', living in Rattlesden Road. Drinkstone National School logbooks record his enrolment as a pupil, sometime between 1885 and 1893, probably in 1889. By 1901, Cecil was 16 and had left school, his occupation given as 'yardman on a farm' (with a later note which reads 'Ag. Cattle'). He and the rest of the Rose family were living at The Green, Drinkstone. In 1911, Cecil was still at home with his parents, brother Sidney and two sisters; the father and both boys being 'labourers on farm'. A report in the BFP of 17th November 1917 stated that Cecil had "*worked for Mr JC Taylor of Drinkstone, practically since he had left school*". (The Kelly's Directory for 1916 lists John C Taylor [born 1863] as 'farmer - Hall Farm'). See also *Family Notes* below.

Like his brother Sidney (*see previously*), Cecil was most probably one of those willing volunteers who attended the meeting at Drinkstone School on 2nd September 1914 and enlisted with his brothers Sidney, George and (later) Walter. Cecil was sent to Shorncliffe Camp in Kent for his initial training, then to Colchester, Salisbury Plain and finally Codford in Wiltshire.

Private Cecil Rose landed in France with the 8th Battalion on 25th July 1915. His military record has not survived, but his movements would have followed that of the other Drinkstone men in the 8th Battalion at the time (*outlined previously*).

Cecil almost certainly participated in the Battle of the Somme, not from the outset but later in July 1916 during attacks on Longueville and Delville Wood. On 26th September, he likely played his part in taking the fortress of Thiepval, with the 10th Essex Battalion. Tragically, at the end of October Cecil was probably quite close at hand when his brother Sidney was killed, blown up by a shell.

Army life, in and out of the front line, wore on for the three remaining Rose brothers in the 8th Battalion through that winter of 1916/17. At some stage, according to the report in the BFP of 17th November 1917, Cecil had enjoyed some home leave, but it isn't clear exactly when. Over Easter in the following April, the Suffolks were in Ham-en-Artois, in the Pas-de-Calais Department, for training. By the end of the month they were on the move, back to the front facing the enemy-held village of Chérisy, some 8½ miles east of Arras.

*British troops en route for the trenches April 1917*

Here they operated in support of attacks carried out by the 54th and 55th Infantry Brigades, which began on the 3rd May.

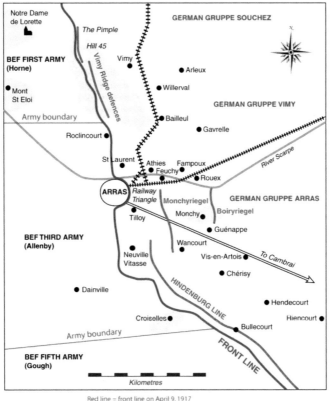

Red line = front line on April 9, 1917
Green lines = Major German trench systems / defensive lines
Blue line = River Scarpe

An account of the attack that day reads, *"in the darkness before the dawn .... long lines of troops were set in motion. The 18th Division attacked with two brigades, one of which (55th) captured Chérisy and advanced to a depth of about three thousand yards. Along the front immediately to the north and south of that village matters had not gone so smoothly, and the 55th Brigade, with both flanks in the air, was forced to withdraw to its original position. While the 53rd Brigade* [including the 8th Suffolks] *in support was moving up in broad daylight and in full view of the enemy, it came under heavy artillery fire, the battalion sustained numerous casualties,* [1 officer, 26 other ranks]. *About noon the Germans counter-attacked vigorously, retaking Chérisy after much bitter fighting and remaining in possession."*

*The ruins of the village of Chérisy*

The Battalion War Diary for 5<sup>th</sup> May 1917 reported, "*10pm: Enemy shelling heavy in front and support trenches. Lieutenant Trounce killed, and 13 other rank casualties*"

The entry for 7<sup>th</sup> May begins, "*Nothing of particular incident occurred during the day*"; no casualties were recorded. However, in the published history of the 8<sup>th</sup> Battalion (1915-1918), it states that on the 7<sup>th</sup> May, Private Cecil Rose died at Chérisy. He has no known grave, but his name is incised on the Arras Memorial (Bay 4). The War Diary is not clear whether Cecil was actually killed on 7<sup>th</sup> May, or whether he was among the other ranks recorded as casualties on 3<sup>rd</sup> or 5<sup>th</sup> May as a result of enemy shelling and died of wounds subsequently. The BFP article of 17<sup>th</sup> November 1917 merely reports, "*Prvt. Cecil Rose (unmarried) was killed in May 1917 whilst taking rations up to the front.*"

The official form reporting Cecil's death would have been delivered to his mother and father in Drinkstone Green shortly after the 7th. On 9th October 1917, Private Rose's outstanding pay - £12 1s. 11d. (£12.10) was forwarded to his father, William as next-of-kin. He received a further £12 10s (£12.50) as a War Gratuity in October 1919. Cecil Rose's service medals – 1914-15 Star, British War Medal, Victory Medal – followed by the Memorial Plaque and scroll, would have been sent to his parents after the War.

As well as being named on the Drinkstone First World War memorial, Cecil is also recorded on the framed 'Roll of Honour' in All Saints' Church. Unhappily for the Rose family, he was not the last of the brothers to lose his life.

*Family Notes*
The BFP article of 17th November 1917, with details about the Rose Brothers killed during the War, mentions that Cecil worked as a farm labourer for JC Taylor. However, he was not the only member of the Rose family employed by John Taylor. The 1911 census includes 28-year-old Eva Elizabeth Rose, Cecil's elder sister, as a servant in the Taylor household at 'The Hall', Drinkstone: the live-in cook. More than this, on 3rd December 1918, John Crumpton Taylor married his former employee Eva at Christchurch, Fulham SW6, a little under half a mile away from 215 Stephendale Road, which was given as her address. On 29th June 1920, a son was born to the couple and named Cecil John (in honour of Eva's brother and after his father?). He was enrolled at Drinkstone School in 1927 and died in Southend, Essex in September 1987. John Taylor died in 1950 and is buried in All Saints' churchyard, Drinkstone; Eva died in Sudbury in March 1956.

# ALFRED HARVEY

6th Battalion, Alexandra (Princess of Wales's Own)
Yorkshire Regiment
Army Number 25299
*KILLED IN ACTION 14th August 1917*

Alfred Jonathan Harvey was born in Drinkstone, Suffolk on 14th April 1892, the third of 4 children of Alfred Harvey, a horseman at Green Farm, Drinkstone and his wife Sarah (née Bullen, born in Denton, Norfolk). The family probably came to Drinkstone in 1890/91, initially to Rattlesden Road, probably to work for farmer Emily Jewers of Green Farm. At some time after 1891, the family moved to Cross Street, into one of three tied cottages once known as Medway Cottages (now a single dwelling called 'Treaclebenders'). Alfred was baptised at All Saints' Church, Drinkstone on 12th June 1892 by the Rector, Frederick Horne.

*'Treaclebenders', August 2017. Courtesy: James Munday*

The young Alfred was enrolled as a pupil at Drinkstone National School in 1896. The census return for 1901 records Alfred in Cross Street with his parents, his two elder sisters (Olive and Mildred) and his brother Frank, two years his junior. By the 1911 census, Alfred (aged 19) was still living with his parents and Frank in the same place and was described as a 'labourer on farm'. According to family accounts, he was known as 'Happy' on account of his habitually cheery disposition.

At some stage after this, Alfred had left home and moved to the north of England in search of work. It seems he volunteered for the army with the Yorkshire Regiment (also known as 'the Green Howards'), probably in about November/December 1915, with his place of residence recorded as Middlesbrough. According to the official Medal Roll compiled in May 1920, he was initially enrolled in the 10th (Service) Battalion with the regimental army number of 25299. Subsequently he transferred to the 6th (Service) Battalion (Alexandra Princess of Wales's Own) of the Yorkshire Regiment, retaining the same number. Alfred's personal service record has not survived and without any definitive evidence we cannot say exactly when Alfred joined the forces, but his approximate enlistment date has been inferred from 'signing up' dates of other soldiers in the same regiment that *are* extant. In addition, Alfred's name does **not** appear on the 'Roll of Honour' that lists those men 'now on active service', (compiled during 1915), that is displayed in All Saints' Church, Drinkstone. At any rate, it is not likely that Alfred served overseas until at least 1916, as records do not show that he was issued with a 1914-15 Star (medal).

After joining up, Alfred would have undergone training in Britain for several months, before joining the Yorkshires in France. The 10th Battalion had landed in Boulogne on 10th

September 1915; the 6<sup>th</sup> Battalion arrived in Marseilles from Egypt on 1<sup>st</sup> July 1916. During September 1916, the 6<sup>th</sup> Yorks suffered severe casualties of around 400 other ranks in actions in the Authuille/Thiepval area of the Somme. It may well have been following these losses that Alfred was drafted in to make up the Battalion's strength. Nonetheless, in 1917 the 6<sup>th</sup> Yorks saw action on the Ancre, then moved to Flanders for the Battle of Messines and the Third Battle of Ypres – also known as Passchendaele.

*Men of the Yorkshire Regiment (Green Howards) cleaning their rifles after coming out of the line, 3 August 1917. Imperial War Museum*

At present, we do not have any details of Alfred's role or experiences during his active service in any of the above engagements. However, according to the regimental war diaries, we know that the Battalion was camped in a wood to the west of Ypres between 1<sup>st</sup> and 7<sup>th</sup> August. On the 8<sup>th</sup>, the 6<sup>th</sup> Yorks moved up into dug-outs at the Yser Canal and busied themselves in working parties and night patrols to reconnoitre enemy positions. On the 13th and early on the 14th, British artillery shelled German positions. At 4am on the 14th, the Battalion formed up on the west bank of the Steenbeek and began to advance towards the enemy.

*Battle of Passchendaele 31 July – 6 November 1917*
*Officially known as the Third Battle of Ypres, Passchendaele became infamous not only for the scale of casualties but also for the mud*

The War Diary account continues,

*"C Coy gained their objective on the left. A Coy held up on the right by hostile MG [machine gun] fire from dug-outs untouched by bombardment. Enemy delivered several small*

*attacks during the day on A Coy which were easily repelled by rifle fire. Intense shelling all day by enemy. At night, battn. relieved by 5<sup>th</sup> Dorset Regiment".*

Casualties listed for the day were: 2 officers wounded, 20 other ranks killed, 26 missing, 63 wounded. One of those killed (or reported missing) on 14<sup>th</sup> August was Private Alfred Harvey. He has no known grave, but his name is inscribed on the Menin Gate Memorial (panel 33) in Ypres.

Family accounts relate that at some stage during his service, Alfred was given some leave back in Drinkstone and foretold *"I shan't be home again".* The sad news about Alfred would have been delivered to his mother and father in Cross Street shortly after the 14<sup>th</sup>. On 12<sup>th</sup> December 1917, Private Harvey's outstanding pay - £13 6s. 3d. (£13.31) was forwarded to his father Alfred, as his next-of-kin. He received a further £7 10s (£7.50) as a War Gratuity in October 1919. Ultimately, Alfred Harvey's service medals - British War Medal and Victory Medal - as well as the Memorial Plaque and scroll were despatched to his parents in Cross Street.

*No photographs of Bertie Phillips have yet been found.*
*This is a Private of the 2nd/5th Battalion Leicestershire*
*Regiment from the Great War period Courtesy: ww1tigers.com*

# BERTIE PHILLIPS

2nd/5th Battalion Leicestershire Regiment
Army Numbers 5910; 242205
*KILLED IN ACTION 27th September 1917*

Bertie Phillips was born in Drinkstone, Suffolk on 18th May 1888, the youngest son of 5 children of Edward Phillips (from Great Barton) and his wife Anna (née Barrell, born in Drinkstone). Shortly after their marriage in summer 1880, the newly-married couple moved to a cottage next door to Anna's parents, Charles and Sarah Barrell, on Drinkstone Green and they were still at the same house until the 1920's at least. In 2005, long-time Drinkstone resident Tom Smith remembered it as being in Cherry Tree Lane (off Gedding Road). Bertie's father was described in the 1881 census as a photographer, in 1891 as a farmer, in the 1901 and 1911 censuses as a waiter (domestic/casual) and on Bertie's birth and marriage certificates as a butler. His mother was listed in all censuses and in Kelly's Directory as late as 1933 as a dressmaker.

Bertie was baptised at All Saints' Church in Drinkstone by the Rector, Frederick Horne, on 29th July 1888 and he was enrolled as a pupil at Drinkstone National School, most likely in the autumn/winter of 1892/93. The 1911 census places Bertie – incorrectly named Albert - (aged 22) living far from Drinkstone, serving as a domestic servant at Burwash Court in the parish of Burrough-on-the-Hill and Somersby, near Melton Mowbray, Leicestershire. The next reference to Bertie is on a marriage certificate for 7th June 1913, the day on which he married Hilda May Chapman, who was 22 years old, at Wandsworth Register Office. She was born in Plumstead, Kent but by 1901 the family was living in the Barking Road, East Ham. The certificate records that Bertie's residence was in Church Street, Kennington and he was employed as a domestic butler; his bride's address was Parma Crescent, Battersea. Just two months later, on 25th August, Hilda gave birth to a daughter, Kathleen Hilda (known as Kitty), in Battersea. She was baptised at St Mark's Church, Battersea on 2nd November 1913 with the address recorded as 34 Parma Crescent.

*44 Aliwal Road, Battersea July 2016*

The Phillips family were living at 44 Aliwal Road, Battersea when Bertie signed up to serve in the 2nd/5th Battalion of the Leicestershire Regiment (originally part of the Territorial Force) on 31st May 1916 and was allotted '5910' as his Army Number. The Territorial Force was renumbered from 1st March 1917 and Private Phillips was assigned a new Army Number - 242205.

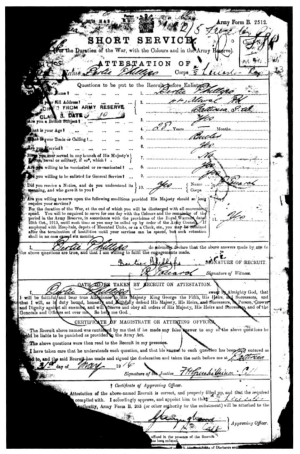

*Attestation form from Bertie's service record*

His army service records have mainly survived and the they reveal that on enlistment, Bertie was 5ft 9ins tall, weighed 124lbs and that his chest, when fully expanded, measured 33½ ins, an expansion of 2½ins. He began his training in Britain from 5th October 1916 and joined the rest of the Battalion on their return from service in Ireland on 7th January 1917.

After a period of embarkation leave, the Battalion proceeded to France via Southampton, arriving at Le Havre on 24th February 1917. From here the Leicesters were sent to the Somme area, where the Germans were retreating to the Hindenburg Line. Bertie would have first seen action in an attack made on the villages of Hesbecourt and Hervilly on the 31st March. Both villages were captured, but at the cost of a number of casualties.

Among the surviving service papers, there is an entry that says that Private Phillips was recorded as a 'casualty' on 5th August 1917 but no further details are given, except that he was sent to the 3rd Army 'Rest Camp' (at St Valery-Sur-Somme) on the 9th August. This was run by the YMCA and might be fairly described (and was by some soldiers) as a kind of 'holiday camp'. Private George Kay of the Border Regiment stayed there in July/August 1917 and wrote in his diary: *"Here I spent a fortnight of absolute rest – the best holiday I have had in France"*. Rubber stamps alongside in the service papers also record that Bertie 'embarked at Folkestone' and 'disembarked in Boulogne' (which seems to suggest that he was back in England before this?). He rejoined his unit on 20th August.

We do not have any further details of Bertie's role or experiences during his active service. However, according to the regimental war diaries, we know that at the beginning of September the 2nd/5th Battalion moved north to Belgium, where training and preparations were made to take part in the Third Battle of Ypres - also known as Passchendaele. The strength of the unit at that time was recorded as being 843 – 27 officers and 816 other ranks.

On the evening of 24th September, the Battalion took over front line trenches at Hill 37, Hill 35 and Elmtree Corner. At 5.50am on the 26th, the Leicesters went 'over the top' under the cover of a 'creeping artillery barrage' and within an hour all objectives had been successfully taken. Later that afternoon, an enemy counter-attack was beaten back. On the following day, 27th

September, the Battalion War Diary reported, *"Hill 37: Artillery on both sides very active during the day. Battn. relieved part of 2/5th Lincolnshire Regiment and part of the 2/5th Sherwood Foresters in the front line"*.

No details of casualties were given, but it is known that Private Bertie Phillips was killed in action that day. He has no known grave, but his name is inscribed on the Tyne Cot Memorial to the Missing (panel 51), north-east of Ypres.

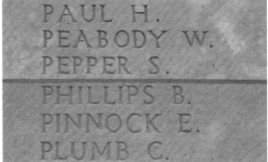

*Tyne Cot Cemetery, near Ypres, and memorial panel*

The awful news about Bertie would have been delivered to his wife Hilda and young Kitty in Aliwal Road, Battersea and relayed to his mother and father in Drinkstone Green shortly afterwards. On 29th January 1918, Private Phillips' outstanding pay - £2 5s. 11d. (£2.30) was forwarded to Hilda, as his next-of-kin. She received a further £3 as a War Gratuity in November 1919 and was awarded a pension of 18/9d. (94p) per week for herself and her child, with effect from 22nd April 1918. Later, Bertie's service medals - British War Medal and Victory Medal - as well as the Memorial Plaque and scroll were sent to his wife in Battersea.

*Family Notes*

As mentioned above, on their marriage Bertie's parents, Edward Phillips and Anna Barrell moved next door to Anna's father and mother, Charles and Sarah Barrell, on Drinkstone Green. Interviewed by Sheila Wright for her book '*Drinkstone School and Village*' published in 2005, Tom Smith (who had moved to Drinkstone in 1920) recalled *"There were two old cottages at Cherry Tree Lane. It used to be one cottage, where PC Barrell the policeman, Pansy's\* grandfather, used to live. They had the other end built on for Pansy's father and mother"*.

*\* Pansy was the name adopted by Anna Elizabeth, the Phillips' youngest child*

Edward and Anna had five children (according to the 1911 census): Edward (born 1882); Diana (born and died 1883); Fred (born 1884); Bertie (born 1888); Anna Elizabeth ~ Pansy (born 1895).

Bertie's parents, Edward and Anna, continued to live in Drinkstone until their deaths (in 1941 and 1944 respectively) and are buried side by side in All Saints' Churchyard. Among the floral tributes received for Edward's funeral was one from Bertie's widow inscribed *'To dear dad in loving memory from Hilda and granddaughter Kitty'*.

Pansy, Bertie's younger sister, was born on 24th March 1895 and lived in Drinkstone all her life. In Sheila Wright's book (*see above*), Nell Cocksedge (who first came to Drinkstone in 1920) remembered that *"She was my Sunday School teacher from 1924 until 1927, when I moved to Hessett. When I came back to Drinkstone in 1947, Pansy was still working for the Church. She was cleaner for umpteen years until it got too much for her"*.

In September 1947, Pansy married Stanley Mayes. Pansy was a stalwart of the village and all her hard work for the community culminated in her unveiling the village sign in 1977 (as the resident who had lived longest in Drinkstone), to mark the Queen's Silver Jubilee. Pansy died on 28th December 1979 in her 85th year.

In Commonwealth War Graves Commission records, printed in the early years after the First World War, Hilda and Kitty Phillips' address is given as 41 Lichfield Road, Boundary Road, East Ham. In the 1901 census, Hilda and her parents (John and Louisa Chapman) were recorded as living at 5 Hockley Terrace, Barking Road, East Ham, so perhaps Hilda and Kitty had moved back to East Ham to live with, or near, her parents in the early 1920's. Kathleen (Kitty) Phillips died a spinster in East Sheen on 11th December 1984, aged 71.

# LEONARD GEORGE ROSE

8th Battalion Suffolk Regiment
Army Number 13926
*DIED 12th October 1917*

Leonard George Rose was born in Drinkstone, Suffolk on 13th January 1883, and (according to the 1911 census) was one of 14 children of agricultural labourer William Rose and his wife Kezia(h) (née Butcher, previously Last). Presumably he was a sickly infant, as he was baptised 'privately' (which usually meant at home, possibly because there was a fear that the child might not survive) on Saturday 24th March 1883. Happily, little Leonard (or George as he was known) *did* survive and he was formally received into All Saints' Church, Drinkstone by the Reverend Frederick Horne, on Sunday 27th May 1883. Drinkstone National School records reveal that George Rose was enrolled as a pupil at some time between 1885 and 1893, probably in 1887.

In the 1891 census, George was 8 years old, living in Rattlesden Road and described as a 'scholar'. By 1901, George was 18 and living at The Green, Drinkstone with the Rose family (numbering nine in all) and listed as an 'ordinary agricultural labourer'. In All Saints' Church on Thursday 12th January 1911, George married Annie Armstrong, six years his senior (although the marriage register says only four!), the daughter of a parish clerk and native of Castle Bellingham in County Louth, Ireland. The 1911 census shows the newly married couple living in a five-roomed house at Woolpit Green. George was working as a horseman at Green Farm, Woolpit at that time, employed by Mrs Mabel Spink. A son, David George Armstrong, was born on 28th August 1911 and another son, William Edward, in late 1913.

When War was declared in August 1914, an appeal for 100,000 volunteers was made. There was a very positive response. George Rose was most probably one of those enthusiastic volunteers who attended the meeting at Drinkstone School on 2nd September 1914 and enlisted with his brothers Sidney, Cecil and (later) Walter. The BFP article about the Rose brothers published on 17th November 1917, reported that, *"After finishing their harvest, they joined up in the 8th Battn, Suffolk Regiment"*. Regimental records suggest that George joined on 2nd September (Army Number 13926).

Along with his brothers, George went to Shorncliffe Camp in Kent for his initial training, before being posted to Colchester in early October. The Battalion moved to Salisbury Plain, followed then to Codford, just south of the Plain.

George Rose was sent on active duty with the 8th Battalion, alongside his three brothers and John Whiting, landing in France on 25th July 1915. The Battalion was instructed in trench warfare before taking up duties at the front near Bray-sur-Somme. It then moved north, close to Albert, where the Suffolks received a 'baptism of fire' in warfare as part of the 53rd Brigade. A published history of the Battalion describes the next period of service as a fairly uneventful time, in a quieter section of the line, which extended into the spring. Early in May 1916, training increased with rumours that a 'Big Push' was coming - the Battle of the Somme.

We do not have information about George's role during the Battle, but he most probably took part in the attacks on Longueville and Delville Wood. He survived these actions, which were followed by more training, before the 8th Suffolks returned to the trenches. On 26th September, along with the 10th Essex Battalion, they attacked the formidable fortress of

Thiepval. It was quickly overrun with the whole garrison being killed or captured, with only light British losses. An impressive victory. After a short period of rest, the Battalion returned to the front, west of Courcelette near Albert, taking turns in and behind the lines for the next fortnight. Sadly, on the 29th October 1916, George's younger brother Sidney was killed by a shell.

How and when George progressed from being a private, then lance corporal, to sergeant we do not know at present, as his service papers did not survive the Second World War Blitz. At some time during his service in France, George was granted some home leave - but he was certainly serving with the 8th Suffolks in France during February 1917.

*8th Suffolks at Boom Ravine, February 1917*

The winter of 1916/17 was the coldest of the War, with temperatures well below freezing ruling out fighting by either side. With a thaw beginning, at dawn on 17th February 1917 a British force, including the 8th Suffolks, attacked the German positions on the Ancre Heights at Boom Ravine, close to Courcelette on the Somme. They encountered many deep, muddy shell holes filled with icy water, terrain that was greatly to hamper the advance. Fighting was fiercer than any the Battalion had known previously, but the objective was gained, thanks to the individual determination and courage of the attacking forces.

Among those who exhibited outstanding courage that day was Sergeant Leonard George Rose, who was awarded the Military Medal for 'bravery and devotion to duty' during operations against South Miraumont Trench.

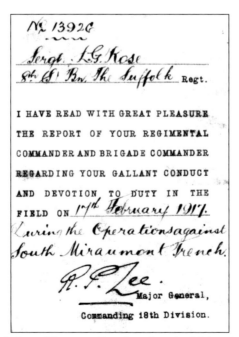

*Commendation of Sergeant Rose's actions by Major General Lee*

In the BFP of 17ᵗʰ November 1917, George's actions were thus described, *"the Battalion next to him was held up by very heavy fire from the enemy. He advanced with a machine gun and discharged a number of rounds into the Germans"*. The printed history of the 8ᵗʰ Suffolks, published after the War, says that Sergeant Rose appeared with a couple of Lewis gunners and soon the position was overcome. The Adjutant wrote later that *"they had the satisfaction of seeing the Germans at once, throw up their hands and surrender."* The BFP report goes on *"Of this achievement he* [George Rose] *modestly wrote: This is what I am out here to do. Anybody else would have done the same, but I was lucky enough to be there at the time"*.

Over Easter that April, the Suffolks were behind the lines for training; by the end of the month they were on the move back to the front and took part in an attack on enemy held Chérisy, 8½ miles east of Arras. Here they operated in support of attacks by the 54ᵗʰ and 55ᵗʰ Infantry Brigades, which began on the 3ʳᵈ May. It was during this battle, on the 7ᵗʰ May, that George's brother Cecil died *"whilst taking rations up to the front"* (as reported in the BFP article of 17ᵗʰ November 1917). To lose a second brother, in the same regiment and battalion too, must have been a very sad blow for both George and Walter, but army life and duty had to go on.

By the end of July, the 8ᵗʰ Battalion had moved north to Belgium, where training and preparations were made to take part in the Third Battle of Ypres (Passchendaele). In the opening battle (of Pilckem Ridge), the 8ᵗʰ Suffolks gave a very good account of themselves, advancing steadily up the Ridge and through Sanctuary Wood, but they had come under heavy fire, suffering 177 casualties. The losses sustained by the Battalion prevented any further participation in the fighting.

After five weeks rest, recuperation and strengthening, the 8th Suffolks were ready again for action. On 9th October 1917, the Battalion formed up on the Yser canal bank north of Ypres, prior to an assault on the German-held village of Poelcappelle. At 5.25am on 12th October a British attack was launched. Regimental histories describe the conditions:

*"A considerable enemy barrage was encountered ... companies had to deploy owing to machine-gun fire" "In a countryside which possessed scarcely one yard of soil without a shell-hole, the continuous rain of a fortnight had resulted in a series of lakes and ponds" "The whole ground was pock-marked with shell-holes, often so full of water, that men had to struggle to prevent themselves from drowning" "In this morass, men lived and slept for three days and nights, lashed by a bitter wind and almost incessant rain; harassed by snipers and shell fire, unable to move by day owing to the close proximity of the enemy, they still managed to keep the line unbroken, even though men were dying from sheer exposure".*

It was in these extreme circumstances that Sergeant George Rose met his end. The BFP of 17th November 1917 reported that George Rose was killed *"whilst taking cigarettes round to the men of his Company whose isolated position had prevented them receiving food supplies"*. That same article also carried the text of a letter written to George's wife by a chaplain attached to the Battalion –

*My dear Mrs Rose – It is with the deepest regret that I write as the Chaplain attached to this Battalion to say how deeply I sympathise with you in the very sad news of the death of your husband, Sgt LG Rose of this Battalion on October 13th (sic) last. He was killed by a bullet while in the act of trying to help his men to better their position in the mud and water in which*

*they were then placed. His death was instantaneously. He was shot through the head and his loss will be felt very keenly by his Company. He was a devoted N.C.O. – able and resourceful and a father to his Platoon. He was very regular at church services and did his utmost to help all he could. You will always have the consolation of the memory of a gallant husband. May God comfort you in this dark hour and time heal these wounds. With very kindest thoughts.*
*Yours very sincerely, Cecil W Deeks, Chaplain, 8th Suffolks*

After vainly striving to advance, any further operations were abandoned. The Battalion had sustained 232 casualties.

The message reporting George's death would have been delivered to his wife Annie and young sons David and William in Woolpit shortly after the 12th October. A memorial service was held at St Mary's Church, Woolpit on the afternoon of Sunday 4th November 1917. The BFP reported that *"the 'Dead March' was played on the organ, and the 'Last Post' sounded by the boys of the V.T.C."* [Volunteer Training Corps].

*Mourning Card given to friends and family*

George Rose is listed on Drinkstone's war memorial plaque and on the 'Roll of Honour' in All Saints' Church. 'Rose LG' is also inscribed on the war memorial in Woolpit, where from 1911 he worked and lived; his life and loss are remembered here too.

Sergeant Rose's outstanding pay - £1 9s. 7d. (£1.48) was forwarded to Annie as his next-of-kin on 9th April 1918. She received a further £17 as a War Gratuity in October 1919. Later, George's service medals – 1914-15 Star, British War Medal, Victory Medal, to go with his Military Medal - as well as the Memorial Plaque and scroll, would have also been sent to his wife.

*Courtesy: Roger Gillespie*

*Courtesy: David Rose*

George Rose was the third of the Rose brothers to lose his life.

**ROSE**—In loving memory of Sergt. L. G. Rose, M.M. 8th Bn., Suffolk Regt., killed in action 12th October, 1917.

The sergeant's voice rang clear and loud :
"Good-night — all's well"

*Bury Free Press, 12 October 1918, one year after George's death*

# WILLIAM EDWARDS

158th Army Troops Company, Royal Engineers
Army Number 216710
*DIED 3rd September 1918*

William Edwards was born in Hoe House Cottage in Gosfield Road, Halstead, Essex on 5th August 1880. He was the eldest of five children of domestic gardener William Edwards (aged 23) originally from Hoxne, Suffolk and his wife Elizabeth (aged 29, née Welch, born in Buriton, Hampshire). William's birth was registered by his father in Halstead on 13th September and he was baptised at Halstead Parish Church on the 29th September. In the 1891 census, William Edwards senior was still working as a gardener, but the Edwards family (now 6 in number, including William junior aged 10, sister Annie, aged 8 and brothers Henry and George, aged 5 and 3) was living in a cottage in Victoria Road, Hoxne. By 1901, with another daughter (Emily aged 9), the family was living in Stradbroke Road, Hoxne but William, now 20 years old, was boarding at 17 Tyler Road, Ipswich with his occupation given as 'bricklayer'.

The 1911 census shows the younger William living back at the family home in Hoxne, his trade still given as bricklayer. The next time William appears in the records, he is marrying Edith Florence Bland at Rattlesden Baptist Chapel on 5th June 1913. Oral family tradition says that William met Flo (as she was known) when she came to work as a domestic servant in the Hoxne area. It may be that William first came to Drinkstone as a result of meeting Flo in Hoxne – or his work as a bricklayer may have brought him to the village in 1912, when the house 'Rolandia' was built in Rattlesden Road *(see below)*. After their marriage, the couple moved into a cottage which Flo already owned (having bought it from a cousin for about £50), in Shop Lane off the Rattlesden Road, now known as Kopsey Cottage.

*Kopsey Cottage, Shop Lane, August 2018. Courtesy: Giles & Daphne Youngs*

The couple soon had two daughters, Kathleen Florence (born in Drinkstone on 23rd March 1914) and Marjorie Helen – known as Molly (born in Drinkstone on 13th October 1915).

Interviewed by Sheila Wright for her book (*'Drinkstone School and Village'*, 2005), Molly told her *"Father was a builder by trade, and he improved the cottage* [Kopsey] *and made it more comfortable. He also helped build a fine large house across the opposite side of Rattlesden Road in front of the Gables* [where Flo's parents Charles and Abigail lived] *... the new house was called Rolandia... now renamed The Homestead. My father owned a horse and trap which were kept at The Gables"*.

*'Rolandia' under construction in 1912. William Edwards is third from left*

The second Military Service Act of May 1916 meant that even married men, under the age of 41, were eligible for call up. Under the terms of the Act, William was 'deemed to have enlisted' on 24th June 1916. He was medically examined on 10th November 1916 and passed 'fit' with 'good' physical development, but with slightly flat feet. William actually signed on in Bury St Edmunds on 1st December 1916.

He was assigned to the Royal Engineers, no doubt to take advantage of his skills as a builder. Over the next 9 months he underwent initial training and service 'at home' and was stationed at Chattenden Barracks near Rochester, Kent. We know that William was at home with Flo and the children in August 1917, from dates inscribed on the backs of photographs. This was probably 'embarkation leave', as from 3rd September 1917 Sapper Edwards was transferred to 'C' section, 158th Army Troops Company RE as a precursor to being sent on service overseas. In this case, service on the Italian front.

*William and Flo with Kathleen and Molly, August 1917*

He embarked on a troopship at Southampton for Cherbourg on 26th September, and then travelled by train to the rest camp at St Germain-au-Mont-d'Or in the Rhone district, arriving on 30th September 1917. Each 'section' was to consist of 61 men, including 48 sappers of which 6 were bricklayers. At 10.30am on 1st October, Sapper Edwards journeyed on with 'C' section to Taranto in the far south of Italy, as part of the joint Franco-British Italian Expeditionary Force (IEF) which was deployed to the Italian front that month.

At present, we do not have precise details of William's role or experiences in this theatre of war (the 'war diary' for 'C' section has not yet been located). However, during her interview with

Sheila Wright, Molly said her father had been in Italy "*building bridges*". According to the Royal Engineers Corps official history (Vol V), both 'A' and 'C' sections were employed as 'lines of communication' troops in Italy. This might include tasks involving water supply, maintaining and developing field defences, gun emplacements, repairing light railways etc – in general, maintaining and repairing facilities. An obstacle faced by soldiers working in a sub-tropical environment like Italy was the summer heat and, in certain marshy areas, the problem of mosquitoes.

Despite being allied to Germany and Austria-Hungary before the outbreak of the First World War, Italy joined the war on the side of Britain and France in May 1915. The first British troops to serve on the Italian front arrived in April 1917, when heavy artillery and supporting Indian logistical units were sent to reinforce the Italian army.

In October 1917, Austro-Hungarian forces supported by German troops went on the offensive, breaking the deadlock. During the Battle of Caporetto, Italian forces were driven back over 100km across northern Italy to within 30km of Venice, to a line along the Paive River. British and French forces were rushed to Italy from the Western Front and elsewhere to support the beleaguered Italian forces and helped stem the tide.

Apart from his initial training in Britain and transit through France, it would seem that William served his whole army career in Italy. By August 1918, the Austro-Hungarian forces were almost spent and being pushed back, and Sapper Edwards was granted some leave. His daughter Molly told Sheila Wright "*while coming home on leave, he contracted malaria and was taken off the train in France*".

William Edwards' service records have survived, including his medical notes. They reveal that he left the troop train at St Germain-au-Mont-d'Or – the very same rest camp at which William and the rest of the 158th Troop Company had stopped on his way to Italy, virtually one year previously. He was taken to Le Manoir Fleurie, being used as a hospital for sick and injured soldiers. William's medical care sheet makes sad and poignant reading. He was admitted to hospital on 29th August 1918 and his notes read ~

*Quite well 1 week ago. Then felt hot. No temp on admission.*

***30.8.18*** *Temp 99°. Sleeps all along. Tongue very dry.....* ***31.8.18*** *Temp normal. Pulse still rapid. No symptoms.....* ***1.9.18*** *Pulse 104. Feels well.....* ***2.9.18*** *Incontinence of urine. Does not eat. Complains of nothing, but speech thick. Temp 101°. Pulse 112.....* ***3.9.18*** *Became unconscious this morning. Conjunctival reflex present. Conj reflex disappears. Right knee jerk absent. Left sluggish. Profuse sweat. Lungs become oedematous. Coma. Death about 6pm.*

Cause of death was initially given as meningitis, but following a post-mortem the next day, this was revised to 'cerebral malaria and necrosis of the spleen'.

A message reporting William's death was sent to his wife Flo and young daughters Kathleen and Molly in Shop Lane, Drinkstone Green on 7th September, informing them that he had died from Meningitis. This was followed by another, nine days later, to say that he had, in fact, died from cerebral malaria.

He was interred in the St Germain-au-Mont-d'Or Communal Cemetery Extension (plot B.15), which is maintained by the Commonwealth War Grave Commission.

*Edward's daughter Molly, visiting his grave, October 1998*

Sapper Edwards' outstanding pay - £9 12s. 7d. (£9.63) was forwarded to Flo as his next-of-kin on 14th November 1918. She received a further £8 as a War Gratuity in December 1919. The Memorial Plaque and scroll would have been sent to her too. William's service medals - British War Medal and Victory Medal - were forwarded to Flo on 2nd March 1922 from the Royal Engineers Record Office.

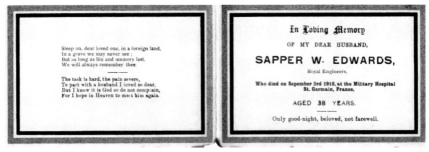

*Mourning Card given to friends and family*

*Letter sent with medals*

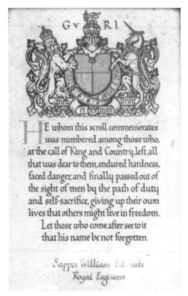

*Scroll sent with memorial plaque*

At 38 years old, William Edwards was the oldest man on Drinkstone's war memorial to have lost his life during the First World War.

*Sapper Edwards during training, Chattenden Barracks, Rochester, 29 Jan 1917*

# DUNCAN VERE WEBB

(3rd Battalion) attached 1st Battalion Leicestershire Regiment
Captain
*DIED 16th October 1918*

Duncan Vere Webb (known as Vere within his family) was born on Friday 20th March 1896 at the Curragh Camp, County Kildare in Ireland, where his father Major Duncan Webb was stationed with the Army Service Corps (ASC). Vere was the eldest of 6 children of Duncan Webb and his wife Madalene (née Brock, born in Glasgow). At the time of the 1901 census, Vere was living with his mother and siblings in Osborne Road, Farnborough, Hampshire, which is close to the ASC Regimental HQ at Aldershot. Shortly afterwards, following Major Webb's retirement from the army on 3rd November 1902 after the end of the 2nd Boer War (in which Major Webb served), the family moved to Drinkstone House in the Gedding Road.

*Drinkstone House, c.1906*

By the 1911 census, Vere was a 15-year-old pupil boarding at Highfield House, Uppingham School in Rutland.

*Duncan Vere Webb 1912. Courtesy: Uppingham School Archives*

He had entered the School in May 1910 and during his time there, he joined the Uppingham Contingent of the Officer Training Corps (OTC), having attained the rank of acting lance corporal by the time he left the School, in August 1913.

*Uppingham OTC, early WW1 period*

In September, Vere applied for admission to the Royal Military College at Sandhurst as an army cadet. According to a report in the Daily Mail on 30th September 1914, he was one of 200 cadets who paraded before the King and Queen, having completed his studies prior to joining a regiment. With war against Germany having been declared just the month before, Vere was 'gazetted' to join the Leicestershire Regiment, his preferred choice and the Regiment in which his father had served from 1881 to 1892.

On 1st October 1914, he was ordered to join the 3rd Battalion of the Leicesters for training at Fort Purbrook, near Cosham in Hampshire. By coincidence, another soldier whose name appears on the Drinkstone War Memorial plaque, Sergeant James Cornish, was already serving with the 3rd Leicesters and was also training at Fort Purbrook during the autumn of 1914. It is not impossible that the two would have bumped into each other here, though NCO's and commissioned officers would not have mixed socially. Just over 3 months later, in January 1915, Second Lieutenant Webb was posted to France to report to the 1st Battalion of the Leicester Regiment (which had been in France since September 1914), in which he served for the rest of his army career.

Precise details of Vere's role or experiences during the bulk of 1915 are not currently available, but by 1st December he was recorded in the Battalion War Diary as being a Lieutenant with 'B' Company of the 1st Leicesters at Poperinghe, near Ypres in Belgium. On the 18th December, the Battalion returned to front line trenches at Wieltje. At 5.15am on the following day, the Germans launched a sustained gas and artillery attack, which lasted for 48 hours. Royal Artillery officers estimated that the Germans had fired 400,000 shells into the area occupied by the British 6th Division alone during this period.

*Christmas card from Vere to brother Hugh, shortly before being wounded*

On 20th December the War Diary reported that *"Lieutenant DV Webb (was) .... badly gassed but did not go to hospital"*. A telegram was received by Vere's father on the 23rd reporting that his son had been 'wounded'; understandably concerned, he had apparently contacted the War Office seeking further information. In reply a further telegram stated: *"...he was admitted 18 Field Ambulance with gas poisoning 22nd Dec and discharged to duty 23rd"*. The truth of the situation subsequently came to light when a report appeared in the London Gazette on 15 March 1916 ~

*"During an enemy attack (19th/20th December) he was not only injured, but buried by the explosion of a shell. Though suffering greatly from shock, he insisted on remaining in command of his company for two days, when his C.O. ordered him to report to the Medical Officer"*. For conspicuous devotion to duty,

Second Lieutenant (temporary Lieutenant) Duncan Vere Webb was awarded the Military Cross for bravery on the battlefield.

**MILITARY CROSS,**

**LIEUT. DUNCAN VERE WEBB.**

Official intimation has been received by Miss Brock, of Baunacora, Loch Lomondside, that her nephew, Second Lieutenant Duncan Vere Webb, 1st Leicester Regiment, has been awarded the Military Cross for bravery on the battlefield. The official statement from the "Gazette" states the Military Cross was won by him "for conspicuous devotion to duty. During an enemy attack he was not only injured, but buried by the explosion of a shell. Though suffering greatly from shock he insisted on remaining in command of his company for two days, when his C.O. ordered him to report himself to the medical officer. The gallant Lieutenant will not be twenty years of age till next week, and he is well known down Loch Lomondside way. He has been at the front since January of last year, and was gassed and slightly wounded earlier in the campaign. His mother is a daughter of the late Mr Henry Brock, of Auchenheglish, Loch Lomondside.

*Lieutenant D V Webb's Military Cross and newspaper report in the Glasgow Evening News 21 March 1916*

After this incident the Battalion was relieved and spent the Christmas period resting in billets behind the lines. DV Webb was promoted to temporary Captain, taking over provisional command of 'D' Company in the absence of another officer in hospital, from 25th December. He was 19 years old.

By 3rd January 1916, Vere was back in the trenches commanding 'D' Company; the War Diary for 5th January states *"German trench mortars active .... Lt DV Webb slightly wounded but remained at duty"*. On the 7th, Vere reverted to the rank of temporary Lieutenant. For the next few months, it was a wearing schedule of deployment in and out of the trenches, both under bombardment and quiet times. A welcome respite must have come for Vere when he was invested with his MC in London, at Buckingham House on 17th May, no doubt with a little home leave. By the 1st June he was back in Flanders, logged in the War Diary as being in command of the intriguingly described 'Forbidden Zone'!

Rather surprisingly, Major Webb (back in uniform for home service) was given special permission to travel to Poperinghe and Ypres at the end of July, presumably to visit his son on active service. In August, the 1st Leicesters were moved to France near Beaumont-Hamel in preparation for an Anglo-French attack due to take place the following month - part of the Battle of the Somme. Lt Webb was kept in reserve with a section of the Leicesters which did not take part in the main attack. During the rest of 1916 and the first part of 1917, Vere remained unscathed. However, on 12th February 1917 he was admitted to hospital with appendicitis and subsequently granted sick leave in England, from 27th February until 20th March.

Vere was listed still absent 'In Hospital' on 1st April, but at 2am on the 18th he was Officer Commanding for a raid on enemy trenches, with the object of 'killing Germans and securing identifications'. An account of the raid in the War Diary says, *'several dugouts blown in containing Germans ... machine gun destroyed ... one prisoner brought back unwounded ... casualties: killed 1, wounded Lt A Wherry, 21 OR's (other ranks), missing Lt A Stevens and 3 OR's; Total: 29'.* Fortunately, Lt Webb returned safely. However, on 6th July he was less fortunate, with the War Diary recording that he was wounded in the trenches – but remained on duty.

Acting Captain Webb retained command of 'C' Company between May and October 1917. Among some surviving family papers is a 'Posting of Officers' notification addressed to him at Drinkstone House (so no longer 'at the front') dated 26th October 1917, informing him that he has been attached to the 2nd Cyclist Brigade in Norfolk! A subsequent letter (dated 30th October) asks him to report to the 1st County of London Yeomanry Cyclists at Melton Constable (roughly between Fakenham and Holt). This may be regarded as comparative 'rest and recuperation' compared to the rigours and dangers of the trenches, but experienced officers were sometimes called home to help with training of new recruits. He remained in Britain for several months – an item in the Leicestershire Regiment magazine from 1918 reports that *"Capt DV Webb MC and Lt PR Milner MC at present on a rest in England are, we understand, attached to the cavalry as instructors"*. For 'cavalry' maybe read 'cyclists'. The 'rest' could not last forever and a telegram dated 17th April was sent to Vere to advise him to report to the Embarkation Officer at Folkestone on the 20th, in order to return to his Regiment in Flanders.

By August, the 1st Leicesters were back in France, first to the St Omer area for training, then on to Holnon in the Aisne Region, where several attacks were launched on German lines in September. During an attack on 23rd September, Vere was wounded again, probably as a result of shellfire. The Germans, now becoming exhausted, were being pushed back, but they still showed stubborn resistance. On 1st October, Vere's promotion to Captain was confirmed. During that month, the Battalion was again in action in the Magny-la-Fosse area, attacking in the early hours of 8th October, advancing and taking ground over the next 4 days. It was during this assault that Captain Webb was shot in the abdomen, possibly by machine gun fire, on the morning of the 10th October.

He arrived at the 5th Casualty Clearing Station the following day, where he was operated on at once, but his wound was serious this time. Nonetheless, Vere was able to dictate a letter to his mother on 14th October, which the padre transcribed and posted for him. In it, Vere reassured his mother that there was no need to worry and that he expected to get home in a week or ten days.

This was not to be. A War Office telegram arrived at the Webbs' summer home in Canford Cliffs, near Bournemouth on 17th October: *'Deeply regret Captain DV Webb Leicester Regt died of wounds Oct sixteenth. Army Council expresses sympathy'.*

The matron at the Clearing Station wrote on the 17th October, '*Yesterday morning he became much worse and died 12am 16.10.18. He did not suffer he slipt quietly away*'. [sic]

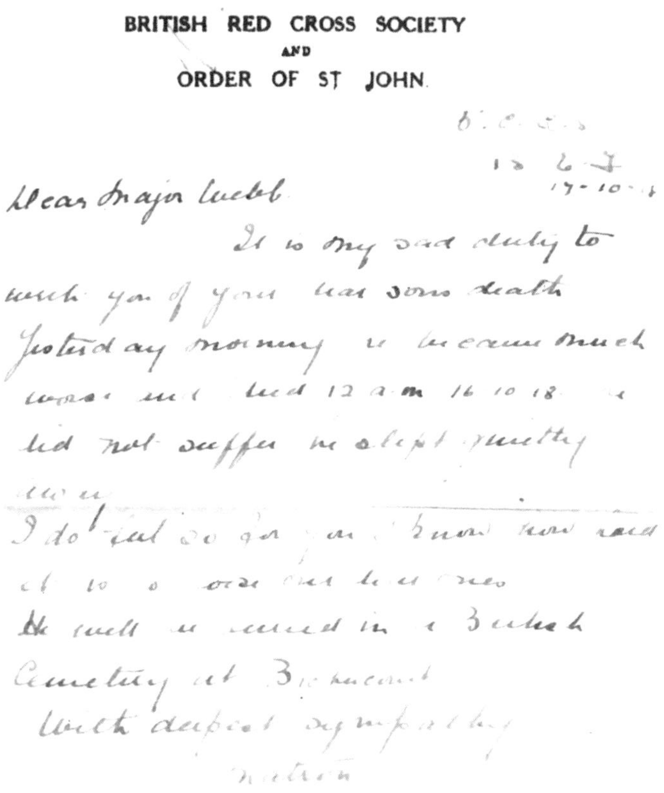

BRITISH RED CROSS SOCIETY
AND
ORDER OF ST JOHN

[illegible]
17-10-18

Dear Major Webb
It is my sad duty to write you of your dear son's death
Yesterday morning he became much worse and died 12 a.m 16 10 18 he did not suffer he slipt quietly away
I do feel so for you [illegible]
He will be buried in a British Cemetery at [illegible]
With deepest sympathy
Matron

Vere was still only 22 years old when he died, but he had seen service in the army for virtually the whole of the Great War. He was buried in the Vadencourt British Cemetery, Maissemy (plot III A. 21).

*Vere's grave with marker prior to official headstone*

In due course, the Memorial Plaque and scroll were sent to Vere's father and mother and his service medals – 1914-15 Star, British War and Victory Medals - were despatched to his father on 28th November 1921 by the War Office.

Duncan Vere Webb is the only commissioned officer listed on the Drinkstone War Memorial. In addition he is listed on the 'Roll of Honour' which hangs nearby. His name also appears on a memorial tablet for officers of the Leicestershire Regiment at Sandhurst and on the War Memorial in the Chapel at Uppingham School.

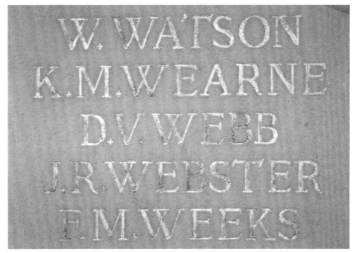

*War Memorial, Uppingham School Chapel*

According to family opinion, Vere's mother Madalene never recovered from her grief. Two of Vere's sisters remained unmarried and in old age Ruth confided to her sister Victoria that each night she dreamed of Vere, in uniform, walking towards her.

The family moved away from Drinkstone soon afterwards, his mother particularly unable to live in a house with memories associated with her lost son.

*Family Notes*

The Webb family moved to Drinkstone in late 1902/early 1903 and began to enter into the life of the local community.

*The Webb children pose at Drinkstone House, c.1910*

Vere's father, Duncan Webb, had been a career soldier, serving as an officer, and was the son of Surgeon General Vere Webb. After attending RMC Sandhurst, he received his commission on 22nd October 1881 and was serving with the 2nd Battalion of the Leicestershire Regiment in 1885. He was attached to the Army Service Corps in 1889 and transferred to the ASC in 1891, and promoted to Captain. He saw service in India, Ireland and South Africa during the 2nd Boer War. He retired, as a Major, on 3rd November 1902.

The Webbs were acknowledged as regular local benefactors, for instance providing evergreens to decorate the church at Christmas 1904 and helping to meet church choir's expenses for an excursion to Great Yarmouth in July 1905. Duncan Webb also served on the Board of Managers of Drinkstone School from 1903 until he left the village in about 1919.

*Drinkstone House interior c.1906*

At the outbreak of the First World War, Major Duncan Webb rejoined the army, aged 52, for home service. From 1917 he was assigned to the 53rd (Young Soldier) Battalion of the Notts & Derby Regiment, which was based in Rugeley, Staffs during 1917. He was one of the two speakers at the recruiting meeting held at Drinkstone School on 4th September 1914 at which 13 men volunteered for enlistment *(see page 4).*

Duncan Webb (senior) seems to have been a somewhat forceful character. He managed to obtain special permission to visit his son at the front in Belgium in July 1916 and following Vere's death, he wrote an angry letter from Hipswell Camp, Catterick to the War Office: *"Sir, With regard to the effects of Capt. D Vere Webb MC, 1st Leicestershire Regt., I beg to inform you that the valise has arrived but it contains nothing but his revolver and a few old brushes and rags. I should like you to inform me what has become of his 2 watches – one a wrist and one a pocket watch – the latter a good one – also what has become of his silver identity disk – which ought to have been forwarded. No field glasses were sent. As an old soldier I can safely say I never saw a more miserable attempt at returned effects. Yrs D Webb Major, 53 Notts & Derby Regiment"*

Despite enquiries being made, it would appear that neither a wristwatch nor field glasses could be traced, but the identity disc and pocket watch were returned with other effects. In a slightly testy reply from Lt Colonel F Latham, Officer Commanding 1st Battalion Leicestershire Regiment, on 28th February 1919, he *"considers that Major Webb's* [final] *comment in his letter ... entirely unjustified"*.

Vere's sister, Ruth, also volunteered during the Great War, as a member of the VAD (Voluntary Aid Detachment) carrying out nursing and general house/kitchen and pantry work. Between 20th April 1917 and 9th September 1918, she worked at Ravenhill Hospital, Rugeley, Staffs; Grata Quies Hospital, Branksome Park, Hants; Greenhill Hospital, Dorset and Finborough Hall Red Cross Hospital, Stowmarket.

# ARTHUR GEORGE PRYKE

13th (County of London) Princess Louise's Kensington Battalion,
The London Regiment
*(previously 8th Battalion, Suffolk Regiment)*
Army Numbers 14901; 483894
*DIED 1st November 1918*

Arthur George Pryke was born in Drinkstone in a cottage near
to Rookery Farm, on 22nd February 1892, the second eldest son
(of six children, five of whom survived), of stockman/groom
Walter Pryke and his wife Kate (née Long), who were both born
in Thorpe Morieux. Arthur's birth was registered by his mother
on 2nd April and he was baptised in All Saints' Church,
Drinkstone on 5th June. Young Arthur was admitted to
Drinkstone School on 7th April 1896, at the age of 4. In the 1901
census, the Pryke family were still living near Rookery Farm,
but by 1911 they had moved to Park Corner and probably lived
at Mead Cottage, Tostock Road – a tied cottage for an employee
of the Reverend Blencowe of The Meade. In the 1911 census
Arthur is described as a 'farm labourer'.

*Mead Cottage, November 2010*

When the First World War broke out, Arthur answered the call to join up – in fact it is quite likely that he was one of the fourteen men who attended a meeting at Drinkstone School on 2nd September 1914 and volunteered for enlistment *(see page 4)*. He joined the 8th Battalion of the Suffolk Regiment in Bury St Edmunds that month and was allocated the regimental number 14901. In company with the other Drinkstone men who had joined the 8th Battalion of the Suffolks, it can be assumed that Arthur Pryke went to Shorncliffe Camp in Kent for his initial training, before being posted to Colchester in early October. After winter exercises, the Battalion moved to Salisbury Plain, and then to Codford, just south of the Plain.

Private Pryke was sent on active duty with the 8th Battalion, alongside fellow Drinkstone villagers Cecil, George, Sidney and Walter Rose and John Whiting, arriving in France on 25th July 1915. The Battalion received training in trench warfare before taking their turn at the front near Bray-sur-Somme, then further north close to Albert. It was here that the Suffolks received their first experience of warfare as members of the 53rd Brigade. The published history of the Battalion describes the next phase of service as being generally quiet, in a more tranquil sector of the front line, which prevailed into the spring.

Precise details of Arthur's role or experiences at this time have not yet come to light, and unfortunately his service records were destroyed during the Second World War London Blitz. However, from dates recorded in First World War medal entitlement records, it seems that his period of active service was interrupted (by wounds, or illness?) between 2nd March and 30th June 1916, and between 16th September 1916 and 5th January 1917. During these periods, Private Pryke was most likely sent back to England to recover.

**THREE DRINKSTONE SOLDIER SONS.**

Mr. and Mrs. Walter Pryke, of Park Corner, Drinkstone, have the proud distinction of having three sons serving their country at the present time. We have pleasure in reproducing their portraits above. From left to right they are: 125 Rifmn. Walter J. Pryke, 3rd Battalion Rifle Brigade, wounded on August 22nd, 1915; 14903 Private Arthur G. Pryke, 8th Battalion Suffolk Regiment, and 13922S Private William A. Pryke, also of the 8th Battalion Suffolk Regiment. The parents of these three gallant sons are to be heartily congratulated on this patriotic record.

*Bury Free Press, 22 April 1916*

After his second period away from the front, he was probably transferred from the Suffolks into the 13th (County of London) Princess Louise's Kensington Battalion, The London Regiment which was to be part of the newly formed 56th (1st London) Division. This was to be made up from battalions that had already served on the Western Front, but whose numbers had been badly depleted and needed to be supplemented from new recruits and others returning after injury or illness. It was thus that Arthur Pryke, a Suffolk boy, became 'a Londoner' in early 1917, with a new Army Number ~ 483894.*

*\* These dates mirror the record of another Suffolk soldier. Private Herbert Ashley, from Brandon, who joined the 10th Suffolk Battalion in 1914 and was wounded in 1916. After recovering in hospital, he returned to duty at some time after October 1916 and was transferred to the 13th Kensington Battalion too, with a new army number – 493887 - just 7 numbers ahead of Pryke's new number, in the same Battalion. Sadly, Herbert was killed in action, a fortnight before Arthur's death.*

Pryke returned to France in January 1917 and seems to have survived all operations and actions with his new unit throughout that year, and the next. During September and October 1918, Private Pryke advanced with his comrades against a depleted and exhausted enemy, helping to capture prisoners, equipment and territory. By October, the Kensingtons were enjoying some respite in billets in Arras. An entry in the Battalion War Diary on 29th October reads *"Owing to an outbreak of influenza, Bttn changed billets in the town and vacated the cellars of the Petite Palace"*. Whether Arthur had succumbed to influenza is unknown; he was probably already in the 24 General Army Hospital in Étaples, near Boulogne by this date. Tragically, having served virtually for the whole War and survived all on the battlefield, he may well have fallen victim to Spanish Flu. Private Arthur Pryke died from what was recorded at first as 'acute bronchitis', later attributed to pneumonia, on 1st November 1918, just 10 days before the Armistice. He was laid to rest in the Étaples Military Cemetery (plot LXVI.N.5).

*Étaples WW1 Cemetery 1919 by Sir John Lavery*

A message reporting Arthur's death was sent to his parents Walter and Kate in Mead Cottage shortly afterwards. His outstanding pay and War Gratuity, amounting to £35 11s. 2d. (£35.56) was forwarded to his mother on 20th May 1919; she received a further £1 12s. 6d. (£1.62½) on 26th July 1919. Finally, the Memorial Plaque (or 'Dead Man's Penny') and scroll *(see pages 163-166)* were sent to her too. For his grieving family they weren't enough: a special commemorative embroidery was commissioned and framed to hang at home in his memory. In around 1998, a Great War enthusiast and collector spotted it on a wet Sunday morning at the Woolpit car boot sale and decided to rescue it from the rain. After a clear-out, he offered it for sale on eBay in June 2009, when a successful bid was made on behalf of Drinkstone to bring it back home. It was skilfully conserved by May Berkouwer and her specialist team in Sudbury, and now hangs in the Village Hall beside his framed 'Penny', which was separately obtained via eBay in August 2016.

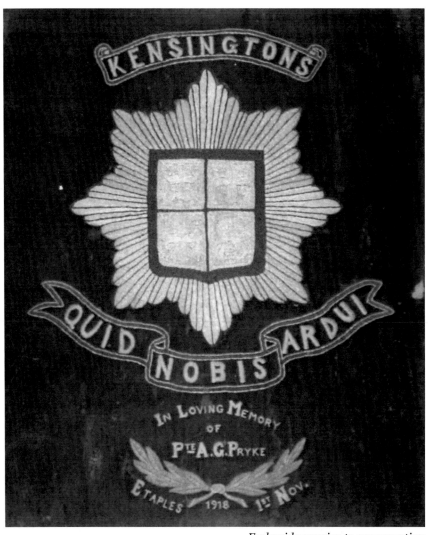

*Embroidery prior to conservation*

The name of Arthur Pryke is not only inscribed on the Drinkstone War Memorial but also on the Roll of Honour for the Kensington Battalion of the London Regiment, that hangs in Kensington Town Hall. He is also recorded on the framed Roll of Honour in All Saints' Church (compiled in 1914/15).

Arthur's older brother, Walter Pryke also served in the army with the Rifle Brigade and his younger brother William with the 8th Battalion of the Suffolks. Both survived the War and died in 1956 and 1991 respectively.

*Arthur Pryke's Dead Man's Penny*

Arthur Pryke is not forgotten in Drinkstone more than 100 years after his death. He was the fifteenth – and final – man from the village to have lost his life during the First World War.

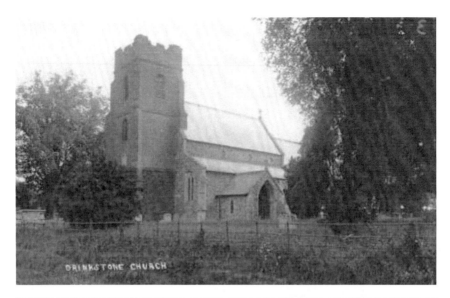

Two Drinkstone institutions: All Saints' Church c.1920 and Drinkstone School c.1980's. Most of the men named in this book were baptised, married or had funerals at the church and attended the school.

# SECOND WORLD WAR

The memorial commemorates the three men who died during, or as a result of service in, the Second World War. It measures 28" (71cms) wide by 17¼" (44cms) high and is made of Portland stone. It hangs below the First World War memorial on the north wall of All Saints' Church. The plaque was unveiled by Colonel Hildesley and dedicated by the Bishop of Dunwich in a special service held at the church on Sunday 16th October 1955. The project to erect the memorial had been overseen by the Drinkstone Branch of the Royal British Legion.

DEAR DAVID & EMILY,

I DON'T KNOW IF YOU REMEMBER WHEN YOU WAS HERE ONE YEAR FOR REMEMBRANCE SUNDAY AND YOU TALKED TO ROBIN SHARP ABOUT PERCY.

WELL HE HAS WRITTEN A BOOK WHICH I THOUGHT YOU MIGHT LIKE ABOUT THE men on DRINKSTONE WAR memORIALS AND on PAGE 134 IS ALL ABOUT PERCY.

I DON'T KNOW IF ALL THE FACTS ARE RIGHT, I HOPE THEY ARE AND YOU ENJOY READING IT.

I BOUGHT THE BOOK FOR YOU BUT SORRY HE PUT MY NAME ON IT, AS IT SHOULD HAVE BEEN YOURS.

LOTS OF LOVE ROSE

# PERCY CHARLES BLOOMFIELD

HMS Pembroke, Royal Navy
Service Number: C/JX 154324
*DIED 21st January 1941*

Percy Charles Bloomfield was born on 26th May 1921, one of 8 children of farm worker Jim Bloomfield and his wife May (née Horrex) ~ Percy, Susan, Gladys, John, David, Dennis, Ivy and William (Billy). He was born in one half of Chesil Cottage in Cross Street, Drinkstone, the other half being derelict. In Sheila Wright's book 'Drinkstone Revisited' (2007) Percy's younger brother David described it as *"one big room, a larder and two bedrooms ... an open range fire ... no running water ... no electricity ... an outside dry toilet"*. It was here that all 10 members of the Bloomfield family lived.

*Front and back views of Chesil Cottage, showing the part in which the Bloomfield family lived.*
*Courtesy: Edna Gunnett*

Percy was enrolled at Drinkstone School in 1926 aged 5, he left aged 14 in 1935 and was employed by Mr and Mrs Gibson-Jarvie of Gedding Hall. Percy joined the Royal Navy when he was 15 and was sent to HMS Ganges, in Shotley, for training. In 1937, while Percy was away in the navy, the Bloomfield family moved from Cross Street to No. 1 of the new Council Houses in Gedding Road, next to the Village Hall.

*No.1 Council Houses, May 2019. Courtesy: Derek Cross*

Percy was posted to serve on HMS Resolution (a Revenge-class battleship), which was tasked to protect merchant convoys in the North Atlantic. Later, according to David Bloomfield, he was employed on minesweeping duties and based initially at Rosyth on the Forth and then at Rothsay, on the Island of Bute in the Clyde Estuary. While serving in Scotland he met a young Scottish girl, Margaret Burton, who lived in Greenock, whom he brought home to Drinkstone for Christmas 1940 and they became engaged.

*Bury Free Press, Jan 1941. Courtesy: Lucy Blake*

Early in the New Year of 1941, Able Seaman Bloomfield was sent on a special training course to HMS Pembroke, a shore-based establishment at Chatham, Kent. While here, Percy fell ill with acute follicular tonsillitis and was taken to the Royal Naval Hospital, Chatham. Complications set in and telegrams reporting on his deteriorating condition were sent home daily to Drinkstone. Sadly, Percy died from septicaemia with his parents at his bedside, on 21st January 1941, aged just 19.

Percy's medals

David Bloomfield recalled that the body of his eldest brother was brought back to Drinkstone and rested, in a coffin, in the front room of No.1 Council Houses prior to the bier being walked to the funeral at All Saints' Church. A local newspaper reported, *"Every token of respect was shown at the funeral on Saturday. The coffin was draped in the Union Jack. The Rev. DE Lilley (rector) officiated at the service and Miss Allen played the organ. The hymn 'Abide With Me' was sung"*. David noted, with disappointment however, that there were no naval representatives present.

Percy Bloomfield was buried in the churchyard in Drinkstone, to the north of the church, and a traditional, white Commonwealth War Graves Commission gravestone was placed above him. The inscription reads: IN LOVING MEMORY OF OUR BELOVED SON "UNTIL THE DAY BREAK".

*Family Notes*

The Bloomfields left Drinkstone for Essex in 1942 so that Jim Bloomfield could find a more steady, better-paid job to support his family. They moved first to Ingatestone and then to Epping and never returned to live in the village. Percy's cousins, the children of his uncle Albert Horrex, Rose and Eddie, still live in the vicinity and tend his grave. Both attend the Remembrance Day service at All Saints' every year and Eddie is a member of the local branch of the Royal British Legion, carrying the standard on ceremonial occasions.

# JOHN MICHAEL HARGREAVES

5th Battalion Grenadier Guards
Lieutenant, Army Number 186891
*KILLED IN ACTION 25th January 1944*

John Michael Hargreaves (known as Michael) was born in Chelsea, London on 15th March 1921, the eldest son of 4 children of John Carne Hargreaves (born 1900) and his wife Angela (née Goschen) who had married in 1920. John Carne's father, John Reginald Hargreaves (born 1864), first moved to Drinkstone with his family, having rented the mansion house Drinkstone Park some time after August 1892, but before March 1895; this was the month and year when John Reginald and wife Bertha's daughter Sybil was born in Drinkstone and baptised at All Saints' Church. The Hargreaves family then relocated to Great Witchingham in Norfolk but, when the opportunity arose, John Reginald bought Drinkstone Park and had moved back by May 1903.

*Drinkstone Park c.1930*

The well-to-do Hargreaves family entered into the life and society of the village, enjoying country life and pursuits and supporting village activities and good causes, through monetary contribution and involvement. For instance, John Reginald served on the Board of Managers of Drinkstone School from 1903 until his death in 1934. He was one of the main landowners in the parish, farming around 200 acres (including Whitefield House and Home Farm). He also bred prize-winning short horn and red poll cattle and had a passion for early motor cars. So much so, he was fined by magistrates in Stowmarket for 'driving a motor car so furiously at Onehouse as to endanger the life and limbs of passengers on the highway' on 28th May 1903. Despite this 'brush with the law', the Hargreaves became a well-known and well-respected family in the village and district. In July 1906 a 'Grand Fete Motor Gymkhana' was held at Drinkstone Park, that raised £200 for the restoration of Hessett Church. The 1916 edition of Kelly's Directory lists John Reginald as a Justice of the Peace.

*Drinkstone Park Motor Gymkhana, 1906, Spanton Jarman Collection*

Meetings of the Drinkstone Girl Guides were held in the ballroom of the mansion, run by one of the Hargreaves' daughters (probably Sybil) who was the Guide Captain; in the 1920's and 1930's, Mrs Hargreaves organised the collections for the Earl Haig Fund (now known as the Poppy Appeal) in the village.

After leaving Eton School, John Carne Hargreaves joined the Grenadier Guards as an officer and career soldier. His young family visited and stayed at Drinkstone Park whenever possible. In conversation with Michael's younger sister Geraldine (Scott-Hopkins) in April 2019, she described how she and her brother Michael loved to stay in Drinkstone during school holidays and developed an affinity for the village and its residents, and the countryside around it.

John Reginald Hargreaves died at Drinkstone Park on 22nd December 1934, aged 70, following an illness which lasted about 4 months. He was buried in All Saints' churchyard. A little after this, his widow Bertha moved to Lavenham, living there until her death in 1951. Ownership of Drinkstone Park passed to John Carne but, as a full-time serving soldier, it seems the family did not live there again, and it was offered for let. However, it would appear that when Major John Carne Hargreaves re-married, to Monica Duncan in March 1939, he brought her to live in Garden Cottage on the estate. According to Sheila Wright in her book *"Drinkstone Revisited"* (2007), he was remembered in Drinkstone as 'Young Jack – a dashing young blade who skilfully landed his private light aircraft in the field between The Park and All Saints' Church!'.

Meanwhile, Michael Hargreaves had followed in his father's footsteps by attending Eton, and on leaving school at the age of 18, he was called up for war service as an officer with the 5th

Battalion of the Grenadier Guards. After training, Michael was sent to the Middle East, taking part in the North African Campaign and in the final stages of the Tunisia Campaign, as a member of the British First Army. The Guards fought significant battles in the Medjez-el-Bab and along the Mareth Line. While serving abroad, as described by Geraldine, he wrote letters and kept in touch with several of the tenant families on the Drinkstone Park estate and farms.

*Grenadier Guardsmen climbing to their forward positions, Anzio, January 1944*

Following the Allied victory in Africa, Michael landed with the Guards at Anzio at the start of the Italian Campaign, on 22nd January 1944. Just three days later, on Tuesday 25th January, Lieutenant Hargreaves was shot by a German sniper as he stood, directing operations from his jeep, and was killed.

According to Geraldine, he had so much enjoyed riding and country sports that his hunting horn was interred with him. He is buried in Anzio War Cemetery, Italy (plot IV, A, 3).

*Courtesy: The War Graves Photographic Project*

In the probate record published later in 1944, Michael's last address was given as 53 Whitelands House, Cheltenham Terrace, London SW3 (near Sloane Square in Chelsea). His effects were valued at £341 0s. 4d. and probate was granted at Llandudno on 3rd May to his uncle (by marriage to his mother's sister) Captain Ralph Eustace Lovett Tennyson-d'Eyncourt of the Coldstream Guards. He himself was to die from wounds received in action in February 1945.

Although Michael Hargreaves was never a full-time resident of Drinkstone, in 1955 when the Drinkstone Branch of the Royal British Legion was planning to place a memorial in the church to honour the dead of the Second World War, the Hargreaves family and in particular the grandson of John Reginald was remembered, and the name M Hargreaves inscribed on the plaque.

*Family Notes*

Michael Hargeaves' grandfather John Reginald was a larger-than-life character who imprinted his character on Drinkstone during some 30 years, a 'presence' that was remembered for many years after his passing. His kindness and concern for his workers was recalled by some of the older members of the village in Sheila Wrights books about Drinkstone (2005 & 2007) and by one, Nell Cocksedge, he was described as being 'stern, but fair'. As mentioned previously, he was an enthusiastic pioneer of motoring. It was said that he drove one of the first five motor cars produced in Britain and was a notable competitor in early car mobility trials.

A list of Drinkstonians serving their country during the First World War, published in the BFP on 9th January 1915, includes 'Hargreaves, JR, Motor Ambulance Red Cross'. It seems that John Reginald was determined to 'do his bit' for the war effort. His name also appears on the 'Roll of Honour' hanging in All Saints' Church (see pages 157-158). In the biography by Des McDougall, 'A Spirited, Stubborn Woman' (2014), about his mother's service during the Great War, is the following passage,

*"Mr Hargreaves, too old for military service himself, answered an advertisement in a national newspaper for drivers and ambulances to join the First Aid Nursing Yeomanry (FANY). It was only when he arrived at FANY HQ for interview that he became aware that the FANY was a women's corps. He was highly amused, and offered himself and his Mors [Torpedo car] to be attached to the FANY entirely at his own expense. He*

*also paid the salaries of two hospital nurses, and for all the petrol used. Becoming known universally and affectionately among the FANY's as 'Uncle", he was a pillar of help and support for them all".*

The car was converted into an ambulance for walking wounded by John Reginald, and driven by him, right into the danger areas. In February 1915, for instance, *"he took Isabel Wicks and FANY colleagues Mary Waite and Muriel Thompson in his car to the Belgium front line armed with woollens and other knitted items, cigarettes and tobacco"* (from 'War Girls' by Janet Lee, 2012). An extraordinary effort!

Meanwhile, back at home, the house had been designated as 'Drinkstone Park Auxiliary Hospital'. [*The Red Cross set up temporary hospitals as soon as wounded men began to arrive from abroad, using a variety of buildings, ranging from town halls and schools to large and small private houses. The most suitable ones were established as auxiliary hospitals where patients were generally less seriously wounded, but needed to convalesce. Servicemen preferred auxiliary hospitals because they were not so strict, less crowded and more homely*]. His daughter Mabel (born 16th December 1893) also served, as a VAD (Voluntary Aid Detachment) nurse, at Devonshire House, Piccadilly between September 1915 and October 1917.

The Hargreaves family had formerly lived at Arborfield Hall in Berkshire and consequently the 'Reading Mercury' carried a report of John Reginald Hargreaves' funeral at All Saints' Church in Drinkstone on Boxing Day afternoon 1934: *"The coffin containing the body was borne in a farm wagon drawn by four Suffolk horses in the charge of work men employed on the estate ... the grave had been lined by Mr A Wright (head gardener) and under-gardeners Cook and Balls from*

*Drinkstone Park with evergreen, arum lilies and Christmas roses".*

Drinkstone Park was advertised to let after John Reginald's death and during the Second World War it was requisitioned by the War Department. It was first used as a Divisional Headquarters and an equipment and munitions depot. It was then occupied by United States troops, mostly black GI's, and later by German prisoners of war. Occupation by the forces resulted in considerable damage to the house, with the American army laying deep, ridged concrete over driveways and some garden paths to facilitate movement of vehicles and heavy machinery. After the War, the Hargreaves did not return to the house and in 1949 it was sold to a speculative buyer. On 12th June 1951 the fixtures and fittings were sold by auction in 150 lots, realising £1,582; the shell of the house was sold for £760 and shortly afterwards it was demolished. The stable block was converted into 2 dwellings and the garden cottage survived. A new house was built in the old walled garden (Little Court) and a bungalow was built in the grounds, now known as The Ambers and currently run as Drinkstone Park Bed and Breakfast.

Michael's youngest brother Jonathan and his wife Veronica lived at Furlong House, in Cross Street, Drinkstone from 1970 until 1987. He, too, was a military man and served as President of the Drinkstone Branch of the Royal British Legion.

ANOTHER SUFFOLK MANSION GOES: Drinkstone Park mansion, near Bury St. Edmunds, the fixtures, fittings and fabric of which were auctioned yesterday for a total of £1,582. The actual shell was sold for £760, and one of the agreements of sale was that it should be demolished in six months.

# GEORGE ERNEST ROSE

Royal Marines
*DIED 25th August 1947*

George Ernest Rose was born in Drinkstone on Monday 30th December 1918, in part of what is now Elm Cottage on the corner of Chapel Lane, which at the time was more than one dwelling.

He was the middle of three brothers, sons of farm labourer Philip Walter Rose of Drinkstone and his wife Alice Mary (née Smith) from Rattlesden. George was enrolled at Drinkstone School in 1923. In 1937 the family moved into No. 5 of the new Council Houses in Gedding Road (later renumbered as 16 Gedding Road).

George joined the Royal Marines in 1937 and 'passed out' on 14th January 1939. According to a press cutting from August 1947, he 'saw service in many parts of the world'.

George's nephew Nigel Rose (who now lives in Drinkstone) recalls his father - George's older brother Philip (known as Walter) - telling him a tale about his uncle during his early war service.

He was serving aboard HMS Southampton, which was laying at anchor off Rosyth on the Firth of Forth in Scotland, when it was struck by a 500kg bomb in an air raid, on 16th October 1939. Official records state that the bomb was released by a Junkers-88 German bomber, flying at below 500 feet. It was a 'near miss' – the bomb hit the corner of the pom-pom magazine, passed through three decks at an angle, exited the hull and detonated in the water. There was only minor structural damage and temporary failure of electrical systems, and the ship was repaired and back on active service before the end of the year.

On 11ᵗʰ January 1941, while engaged on Malta convoy duties (code-named 'Operation Excess') in the Mediterranean en route to Piraeus, HMS Southampton was attacked by 12 German Stuka dive-bombers south-east of Malta. In an interview with Sheila Wright, quoted in her book *'Drinkstone School and Village'* (2005), brother Walter recalled,

*"George got sunk on HMS Southampton, he was in the water seven hours before he was fished out. He was on the cross-turret up the top of the ship with the guns, and he saw these Italian planes coming right out of the sun and they dropped four bombs on the ship. It was a place called 'Hell's Gate' in the Med."*

More formal accounts vary slightly from Walter's version of events. For instance, Luftwaffe diaries describe a squadron of German Stukas, guided by a Heinkel 111 pathfinder, attacking HMS Southampton at extreme range from Sicily, some 300 miles out. The report states that they attacked out of the sun and a bomb exploded in the engine room. 'Official' British reports say that at least two delayed-action bombs hit the Southampton, which caught fire and the resulting blaze spread from stem to stern. The ship was heavily damaged and without power, so the decision was taken to scuttle her, in case she fell into enemy hands. She was sunk by a torpedo fired from HMS Gloucester and four from HMS Orion. A total of 81 men had been killed, but the survivors were picked up by HMS Gloucester and HMS Diamond. According to his nephew Nigel, George was rescued and taken to a military hospital in Alexandria.

Walter told what happened next,

*"They couldn't get George home because of the fighting, so he ended up convalescing two years in Durban, South Africa. He had a shattered left arm …. it was bent, fingers all jammed up. He had contracted TB".*

Photographs in his nephew Nigel's possession show that he spent time at the Oribi Military Hospital in Pietermaritzburg, Natal.

*George Rose, third from left, while convalescing in South Africa (with actress Valerie Dobson in the centre). Courtesy: Nigel Rose*

George did come home to Drinkstone eventually but, according to Nigel Rose, apparently not until after hostilities had ended. His health had been broken and he did not see active service again. A newspaper article published in August 1947 reported that George had undergone a total of 20 operations for the removal of shrapnel. Long-term resident of the village, Cora

Munford (who moved to Drinkstone in 1939 and died in 2016) remembered George living in a wooden hut in the garden of a house, near the Cherry Tree pub (now 16 Gedding Road), that was mounted on a turntable so that it could be turned towards the sun. In conversation with members of the Royal British Legion (RBL) Drinkstone Branch in 2012, it was suggested that the RBL had funded the turntable. Exposure to fresh air and sunlight, to help boost the body's immune system, was considered a helpful treatment for tuberculosis (TB) in the 1940's and earlier, before the discovery of effective antibiotics.

*No.5 Council Houses (now 16 Gedding Road, 2009)*
*George's wooden hut and turntable were mounted on what is now the drive*

George Rose's health was never restored, despite the regime of fresh air and sun. Sadly, he passed away at home, No. 5 Council Houses, on 25th August 1947 aged 28. The cause of death was recorded as pulmonary tuberculosis, brought about it was believed as a result of military service during the Second World War. His profession, at the date of death, was recorded as 'groom'. The probate record, relating to George's 'estate', published on 13<sup>th</sup> December 1947, shows that it was valued at £359 10s 6d.

Details about George's funeral were given in a local newspaper, published in August 1947. The funeral took place at All Saint's Church, with the Reverend Lilley officiating. The hymns sung were 'Eternal Father Strong to Save' and 'Abide With Me'. The Royal British Legion formed a Guard of Honour consisting of Captain Wilson RN (chairman), A Bland (vice chairman), C Pollard, A Horrex, W Hovells, W Steggalls, AH Munford and W Wilding. There is no headstone to mark George Rose's final resting place, but Nigel remembers his father Walter standing on the eastern edge of the churchyard saying, *"This is where brother George is"*.

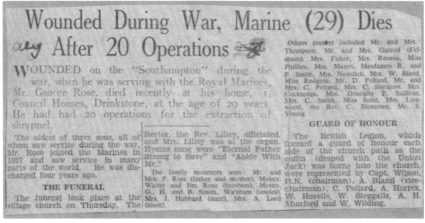

*Press cutting, August 1947. Courtesy: Lucy Blake*

George Rose was the eighteenth and final Drinkstone man, listed on the village war memorials, to die as a result of service in the World Wars.

# Drinkstone Roll of Honour

Just a few feet away from the War Memorial plaques, on the north wall of All Saints' Church, hangs a framed, hand-written 'Roll of Honour' dated 1914-15 that lists 42 men of Drinkstone who 'are now on active service for their King and country'.

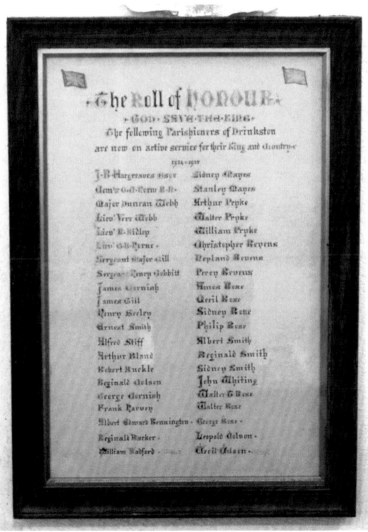

*Approximate size 18" x 13" (46 x 33 cms)*

The text reads:

## GOD SAVE THE KING

The following parishioners of Drinkston [sic]
are now on active service for their King and country
1914-15

| | |
|---|---|
| HR Hargreaves ASDV | Sidney Mayes |
| Comder AA Horne RN | Stanley Mayes |
| Major Duncan Webb | Arthur Pryke |
| Lieut Vere Webb | Walter Pryke |
| Lieut R Ridley | William Pryke |
| Lieut CB Horne | Christopher Revens |
| Sergeant Major Gill | Repland Revens |
| Sergeant Henry Gobbitt | Percy Revens |
| James Cornish | Amos Rose |
| James Gill | Cecil Rose |
| Henry Seeley | Sidney Rose |
| Ernest Smith | Philip Rose |
| Alfred Stiff | Albert Smith |
| Arthur Bland | Reginald Smith |
| Robert Buckle | Sidney Smith |
| Reginald Colson | John Whiting |
| George Cornish | Walter T Rose |
| Frank Harvey | Walter Rose |
| Albert Edward Bennington | George Rose |
| Reginald Barker | Leopold Colson |
| William Radford | Cecil Colson |

```
DRINKSTONE
Horne, Commander C. C., R.N.
Ridley, Sergt. R., Suffolk Yeomanry.
Horne, Sergt. G. B., ditto.
Gobbitt, Sergt. H., ditto.
Bland, A., ditto.
Gill, Sergt., Suff. Regt.
Seeley, H., ditto.
Gill, J., Kitchener's Army (Suffolks).
Pryke, W., ditto.
Cornish, G., ditto.
Whiting, J., ditto.
Smith, S., ditto.
Revens, P., ditto.
Hervey, F., ditto.
Rose, C., ditto.
Buckle, ditto.
Revens, C., ditto.
Mayes, S., ditto.
Rose, G., ditto.
Rose, P., ditto.
Revens, N., ditto.
Colson, R., ditto.
Pryke, A., ditto.
Smith, E., R.E.
Smith, P., R.A.
Pryke, Walter, Yorkshire Regt.
Stiff, A., Lincolnshire Regt. (prisoner).
Hargreaves, J. R., Motor Ambulance Red
    Cross.
Webb, Major, Leicestershire Regt.
Webb, Lieut. Vere, ditto.
```

The BFP of Saturday 9th January 1915 also carried a similar 'Roll of Honour'. Sadly, several of the names included on the Rolls were to be inscribed later on the Drinkstone War Memorial. Other men had yet to join the colours – those listed were merely the ones who had joined during the first year of the war. There were many who returned home after the end of hostilities, but not necessarily 'safe and sound'. These, and others also served.

# Breaking the News

Once a man was confirmed dead, the next of kin were informed of the terrible news. Officers' next of kin were notified by telegram, the next of kin of 'other ranks' were told by receipt of a standard War Office Army Form, B104-82.

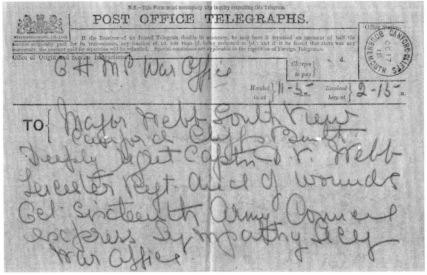

*Telegram informing Captain DV Webb's father of his death*

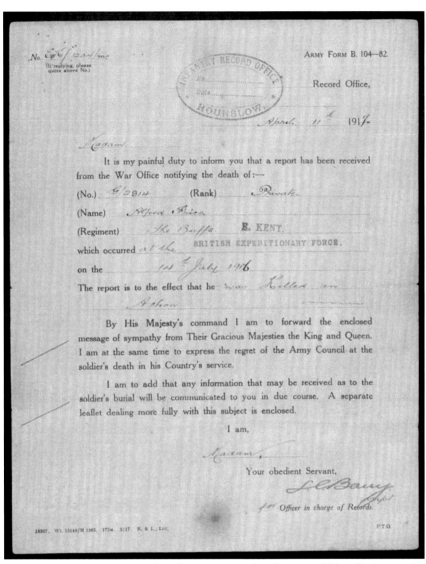

No. _____ (If replying, please quote above No.)

ARMY FORM B. 104—82.

INFANTRY RECORD OFFICE
No. _____
Date _____
HOUNSLOW

Record Office,

_April_ 11th 191_7_.

_Madam,_

It is my painful duty to inform you that a report has been received from the War Office notifying the death of :—

(No.) _G/2914_     (Rank) _Private._

(Name) _Alfred Price._

(Regiment) _The Buffs._   E. KENT.

which occurred _at the_ BRITISH EXPEDITIONARY FORCE.

on the _14th July 1916_

The report is to the effect that he _was Killed in Action_

By His Majesty's command I am to forward the enclosed message of sympathy from Their Gracious Majesties the King and Queen. I am at the same time to express the regret of the Army Council at the soldier's death in his Country's service.

I am to add that any information that may be received as to the soldier's burial will be communicated to you in due course. A separate leaflet dealing more fully with this subject is enclosed.

I am,

_Madam,_

Your obedient Servant,

_J. C. Barry Capt_

_for_ Officer in charge of Records.

18307. W.L. 15148/M 1365. 175M. 2/17. R. & L., Ltd.      P.T.O.

_Standard War Office form B104-82 for the next-of-kin of 'other ranks'_

The ominous official War Office envelopes bearing the bad news were delivered to next-of-kin in Drinkstone from the Post Office, which at the time of the First World War was situated at Blacksmith's Corner. The postmistress was Anna Craske, but it seems that the person who bore some of the brunt of breaking the distressing news to relatives was Mrs Ada Frost of Drinkstone. Her obituary, which appeared in the BFP on 26th August 1933, said *"We regret to record the passing of one of Drinkstone's most respected parishoners in the person of Mrs A A Frost, whose death occurred at her son's residence in Cross Street.... It will be remembered by many of the residents that during the war, Mrs Frost was engaged by the Post Office for the delivery of telegrams, and this duty she carried on for ten years and it brought her in close contact with nearly every resident."*

*Drinkstone Post Office at about the time of the First World War*

# Memorial Plaque and Scroll

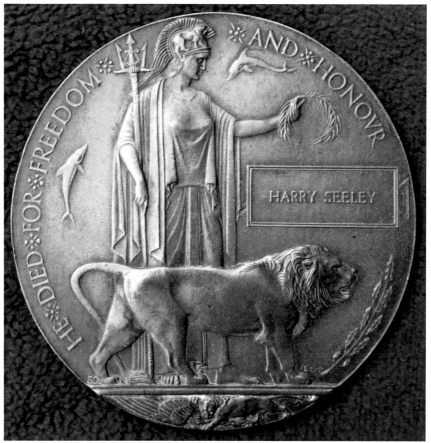

*The Memorial Plaque issued to the next-of-kin of Private Harry Seeley*

The history of the Memorial Plaque or 'Dead Man's Penny' began in 1916, with the realisation by the British Government that some form of an official token of gratitude should be given to the fallen service men and women's bereaved next of kin. The enormous casualty figures not anticipated at the start of WWI prompted this gesture of recognition. In 1917, the government announced a competition to design a suitable plaque with a prize of £250.

There were 800 entries from all over the Empire, the Dominions, and even from the troops on the Western Front. Mr E. Carter Preston of Liverpool, England, was the eventual winner. His initials ~ E.CR.P. ~ were incorporated above the foot of the larger lion depicted on the plaque.

The selected design was a 5" (12cms) disc cast in bronze gunmetal, which incorporated the following: an image of Britannia (symbolising British Imperial power and unity), her head bowed in respect of the named individual, holding a laurel wreath (to celebrate victory) in her left hand and Poseidon's trident in her right hand with two dolphins nearby, (to represent Britain's sea power); a spray of oak leaves and acorns (to signify strength and endurance); at her knee is a lion, defiant and menacing (representing the strength of Britain and the Empire); below their feet is an eagle (the emblem of the German Empire) being torn to pieces by another lion. On the right-hand side is a rectangular tablet, within which the deceased individual's name was cast in raised relief, achieved by a rather labour-intensive process. Any reference to rank was deliberately omitted, to demonstrate equality in each and every sacrifice. On the outer edge of the disc are the words, 'He (or She) died for freedom and honour'.

The relative named as next of kin in a serviceman's service record was sent a form (W.5080) for completion, to be certified by a minister or magistrate, in order to confirm the identity and status of the person to whom the plaque and scroll should be sent. The plaques were packaged in stiff cardboard wrapping, folded like an envelope and marked 'On His Majesty's Service'.

The memorial plaque was to be accompanied by a memorial scroll, a letter from Buckingham Palace and often a letter from the deceased's commanding officer. In many cases, the plaque and scroll (and sometimes a letter from the deceased commanding officer) did not arrive together and were received by families a significant time apart.

## MEMORIAL SCROLL

A scroll, 10½" x 6½" (27cms x 17cms), made of slightly darkened parchment headed by the Royal Coat of Arms was packed separately in a cardboard tube 7¼" (18.5cms) long, with a carefully chosen passage written in old English script ~

'He whom this scroll commemorates was numbered among those who, at the call of King and Country, left all that was dear to them, endured hardness, faced danger, and finally passed out of sight of men by the path of duty and self-sacrifice, giving up their own lives that others may live in freedom.
Let those who come after see to it that his name be not forgotten.'

Beneath this passage, written in the same style, was the name, and rank and service details (including any decorations awarded) of the deceased. To accompany the scroll, again in old English script, was a letter in its own envelope with a personal message from King George V, which said:

'I join with my grateful people in sending you this memorial of a brave life given for others in the Great War'

*George R I*

The scrolls were produced slightly differently, depending on the branch of the services in which the deceased had served. Those in the Army had a large blue H in the main text, with the rank/name/regiment handwritten in red ink; those in the Navy had a large red H and naming in blue ink; those in the Air Force had a large black H with naming in red and blue ink.

Production of the plaques and scrolls, which was supposed to be financed by German reparation money, began in December 1918 at the Government's Memorial Plaque Factory in Acton. In December 1920, production was moved to Woolwich. Approximately 1,150,000 plaques were issued (600 to women), using a total of 450 tonnes of bronze, and continued to be issued into the 1930's. They commemorated those who fell between 4 August 1914 and 10 January 1920 for home, Western Europe and the Dominions, whilst the final date for the other theatres of war or for those died of attributable causes was 30 April 1920.

Unfortunately, the production and delivery of the plaques was not a complete success and the scheme had ended before all the families or next of kin of the deceased received the official recognition that was due. The plaques were popularly known as the 'Dead Man's Penny', 'Death Penny' or 'Widow's Penny', because of the similarity in shape and design to the reverse (or 'tail') of the penny coins of that time.

*Obverse of a penny from 1918*

# First World War Campaign Medals

**The 1914 Star, British War Medal and the Victory Medal**

After the First World War, three medals were awarded to most of the British service personnel who had served from 1914 or 1915. They were the British War Medal, the British Victory Medal and either the 1914 Star or the 1914-15 Star. They were irreverently referred to as 'Pip, Squeak and Wilfred', named after a long-running British newspaper strip cartoon published in the Daily Mirror (as well as the Sunday Pictorial) from 1919 to 1956. By convention, all three medals were worn together and in the same order from left to right when viewed from the front.

Those who had served under fire in France or Belgium between 5 August and 22 November 1914 also qualified to receive a clasp for the Star (together with small silver heraldic roses, to be sewn into the medal ribbon, when just that was being worn), which was instituted in 1919.

For those who did not survive the War, the medals were sent to their next of kin.

# Drinkstone War Memorial Institute (Village Hall)

Even before the end of the Great War, villages, towns and cities throughout the British Isles began to discuss how those who fell during the conflict should be remembered. The residents of Drinkstone also had such discussions. Although, at present, no written record has come to light, it was evidently decided that a village hall should be built to serve as Drinkstone's official War Memorial.

On 30th July 1920, the Ministry of Munitions (by direction of the Disposal Board, Huts and Building Materials Section) held an auction at the former Elmswell Airfield (sometimes referred to as Great Ashfield).[*1] One of the huts on the site (an officers mess cookhouse block of 75 [Home Defence] Squadron, RFC) with dimensions of approximately 71ft by 29ft, corresponds to the dimensions of what became the Drinkstone War Memorial Institute (Village Hall).

According to local accounts 'an officers dining hall from the airfield at Great Ashfield was brought to Drinkstone in sections by horse and cart', at some time between 1920 and 1922.[*2]

*"My father was in the First World War. He remembers how the Village Hall was brought here from Ashfield, on a horse and wagon! My father put some money towards that, it was put there as a Memorial Hall. That was a gift, it was given as a Memorial, so that name shouldn't be changed."* [*3]

In 1921, a piece of land (Elm Tree Meadow) in Drinkstone was bought from Mr Thompson of Rookery Farm for around £26[*4] for the purpose of erecting a village hall as a war memorial for the parish *(see section from Charity Commission document* *below).* The parish priest, The Reverend Francis Herbert Horne, played a prominent role in this project.

The former officers mess was re-erected and dedicated as the official village War Memorial. The earliest documentary evidence of its community use discovered so far, is in the BFP of Saturday 11th March 1922. A report refers to *"A social held in the newly-opened Memorial Hall"* that raised £9 11s with an attendance of around 130 people.

A minute book recording the management committee meetings between January 1928 and January 1969 came to light in September 2016 and refers to activities in the hall from at least 1927.

The hall occupies a special place in the hearts of generations of Drinkstone villagers and others further afield. It witnessed numerous family, community and national celebrations over the years, including weddings, dances, fund-raising events, coronations and other royal occasions. During the Second World War, American servicemen based locally used the hall for various events too, including 'hops' where musicians from the legendary Glenn Miller Orchestra played. In 1951 a charitable trust was established to administer the village hall on behalf of the community *(see below).*

A potentially catastrophic fire at the hall in September 2010, caused by an electrical fault, damaged the front end of the hall and prematurely brought it's working life to an abrupt halt. Up to that point the hall had been well used by the local community, almost on a daily basis. In the search for a new home for the hall, enquiries were addressed to various aviation museums and enthusiasts across southern England. The Stow

Maries Aerodrome Museum expressed an interest in re-erecting the building at their site.

The building was carefully dismantled during April 2011, with the major part of the cherished old village hall being saved. At least five of the six roof trusses were salvaged, and the majority of the walls and floor sections were in good enough condition to be kept. A party of volunteers from Stow Maries arrived at 9am on Sunday 5th June 2011 and it took them some seven hours to completely fill two large lorries. The 'move' was featured on BBC TV's 'Look East' that evening. Disappointingly, the Stow Maries Museum did not fulfil the undertaking that was made to re-erect the hall at their site, potentially as an educational area for schools, and the parts remained stacked in the open in the grounds of the museum.

In 2016 a message was received from Taff Gillingham, one of the team behind the Great War Huts project at Hawstead, west of Bury St Edmunds, to say that Stow Maries had given them the old village hall for re-erection at their site to be one of the buildings displayed there – under 10 miles from Drinkstone! Very sadly, a subsequent message from Taff revealed that the building sections had been left uncovered in Essex and most of the best timbers had been robbed to repair other buildings at Stow Maries. Little remained – no more than a tenth of the original and not one single window.

There is one chink of light in this tale of the sad demise of Drinkstone's original War Memorial Institute. Taff has asked the Planning Officer if the remains of the village hall might be used as the basis for the café on the site. It would not be a complete hut by any means, but at least if permission is granted, Drinkstonians will be able to have a cup of tea and a piece of cake in what is left of the old Institute.

Meanwhile a modern replacement was opened at the original location in July 2013. The new Drinkstone War Memorial Institute flourishes and still serves as a busy social hub for the village, ensuring that those who died in two World Wars are still remembered by succeeding generations of Drinkstonians.

*1   *Notice in the 'Press and News', Friday July 16th 1920*

*2   *This date awaits further verification*

*3   *Ernest Revens: 'Drinkstone School and Village' by Sheila Wright (2005) p.102*

*4   *Dennis 'Sooty' Bradley: 'Drinkstone School and Village' by Sheila Wright (2005) p.162*

## CHARITY COMMISSION

Scheme including appointment of Trustees and vesting in Official Trustee of Charity Lands (sealed 6th November 1951)

In the matter of the Charity called THE DRINKSTONE WAR MEMORIAL INSTITUTE, in the Parish of DRINKSTONE, IN THE county of SUFFOLK, comprised in a conveyance dated the 31st March 1921 and a declaration of trust dated the 1st April 1921

FIRST SCHEDULE

Land containing three roods or thereabouts part of a meadow known as Elm Tree Meadow situate in the Parish of Drinkstone and numbered 240 (part) on the Ordnance Survey map being the land comprised in a conveyance dated the 31st March 1921 made between the Norwich Life Assurance Company of the first part William Edward Dannatt of the second part and The Reverend Francis Herbert Horne and two others of the third part with the building thereon used as a village institute.

*Drinkstone War Memorial Institute c.1940*

*Drinkstone War Memorial Institute 2014*

*The Memorial Wall in the new Institute 2018*

# The Great Influenza Pandemic
## 1918-1920

In January 1918, a new belligerent entered the War – but took no particular side. This enemy was a virulent form of influenza (colloquially, but erroneously, known as 'Spanish Flu'), the first of the two pandemics involving the H1N1 virus that spread throughout the World during the following 2 years. An estimated 500 million people were affected, and it resulted in the deaths of some 50 to 100 million people (three to five percent of the world's population), making it one of the deadliest natural disasters in human history.

The pandemic spread quickly, and claimed the lives of thousands of soldiers many of whom had survived the bullets and the shells during four years of a terrible war. Usually, children and old people are most at risk during flu epidemics, but many victims of this virus were young adults. One explanation put forward being that older generations had built up better resistance through having survived an epidemic 20 years earlier. The majority of those who fell ill with the flu during the spring of 1918 survived, but the virus mutated to a far more deadly strain later that year, into one that could kill within days. The initial symptoms were: fever, headache, sore throat and a cough; this frequently developed into pneumonia which resulted in a blue tinge to the lips, indicating that the victim's lungs were filled with mucus or blood. Death usually followed within 24/48 hours.

The biggest staging camp and field hospital in France, at Étaples, was identified as being at the centre of the Spanish Flu pandemic following research published in 1999 by a British team, led by virologist John Oxford.

In late 1917, military pathologists had reported a new disease with high mortality that they later recognised as the flu. The overcrowded camp and hospital, which treated thousands of casualties, was an ideal site for the spreading of a respiratory virus - 100,000 soldiers were in transit through the area every day. There was also a live piggery and poultry were regularly brought in for food supplies from surrounding villages. Oxford and his team advanced the theory that a significant precursor virus, harboured in birds, mutated and migrated to pigs.

It was just this that seems to have taken the life of Private Arthur George Pryke at the 24th General Hospital at Étaples, who died from what was recorded at first as 'acute bronchitis', later attributed to pneumonia, on 1st November 1918, 10 days before the Armistice.

# Cigarettes and Smoking at the Front

Viewed from the 21st century, with our contemporary outlook and views about smoking, it may seem that George Rose's death on the 12<sup>th</sup> of October 1917 - shot by a sniper while distributing cigarettes to his comrades - was particularly unnecessary, futile and tragic. However, consider the circumstances of the time: soldiers were under incessant fire, marooned in muddy, water-filled shell-holes, lashed by a bitter wind and almost constant rain for several days and nights. In the face of these extreme conditions, Sergeant Rose sought to bring comfort and solace by taking cigarettes to the men of his Company whose isolated position had prevented them from receiving food supplies and paid with his life.

We should try to reflect on George Rose's actions (and consequent death) in the context of the times and with historical perspective. In 1917, the majority of adult men in Britain were smokers. Smoking was not merely a fashion, but part of everyday life - it was what men did. It was not looked upon as 'a filthy habit', nor recognised as injurious to health, or regarded as unacceptable by society in general.

Cigarettes or 'smokes' were a real lifeline for the soldier, invariably hanging from the lip of the archetypal British Tommy. Cigarettes were one of the most frequently requested comforts for men of all ranks at the Front. An officer observed *"If the men can only get a 'fag' or a pipe they are content. They pay no heed to discomfort in the trenches or on the march in the worst weather. Even if they are without their rations, they won't complain if fags don't fail".* (from *'The Bystander'* magazine).

Tobacco rations, aimed at boosting morale and calming nerves, were introduced to the forces in 1916. When Princess Mary sent her famous Christmas Gift Box to all those on active service in December 1914, along with a Christmas card and a photograph of the Princess, it contained an ounce of tobacco plus a packet of cigarettes.

'ARF A MO KAISER!'

One of the most recognised cartoons of the War shows a Tommy in full-service kit, lighting up in the front line with the caption 'Arf a Mo Kaiser!' In other words, even the Kaiser himself could not come between the irrepressible British soldier and his smokes.

Between enemies, often the ultimate display of compassion was to offer a cigarette to prisoners and the wounded.

The superstition known as 'three on a match' was probably current during the First World War – and possibly in earlier conflicts. The belief was that it was bad luck for three people to share a light from the same match. The fear was that the first cigarette lit would catch a sniper's eye; the second would let him take aim; the third would allow him to pull the trigger and find his mark. Indeed, the celebrated Edwardian short-story writer known as 'Saki' (Hector Hugh Monroe) - a Lance Sergeant in the London Fusiliers – was killed by a sniper in No-Man's-Land near Beaumont on the Somme in November 1916. Fearful that cigarette smoke might alert the enemy to their position, his cautionary order to one of the soldiers sheltering with him in a muddy and flooded crater to *'Put that bloody cigarette out!'*, merely drew the fatal attention of a German sniper and a bullet to the head ended his life.

A century on, smoking is accepted as being a killer, but during the Great War cigarettes were an essential commodity for British servicemen. Perhaps considering the dangers faced on a daily basis by those at the Front, it's possible that, had the men in the trenches known then what we know now about the risks and hazards of tobacco consumption, it may not have made the slightest difference to them.

# Acknowledgements

Having spent over a decade researching the lives and times of the men and their families in this book, and of Drinkstone in general during the first half of the 20th century, I have contacted and met many people who helped me and who provided fascinating and valuable information. I warmly acknowledge this help and thank everyone who has generously given me encouragement and assistance in so many ways. Of course, I know full-well that naming individuals or organisations in print will inevitably leave me open to the likelihood of omission, or expose the forgetfulness of advancing age. So, I apologise here and now to anyone I may have missed out. I assure you that it is not deliberate, nor because your contribution has not been worthy. Sorry! Despite this, I would like to sincerely thank (and it's a long list!):

Gwyn Thomas, former Curator of the Suffolk Regiment Museum (for his patience and for being my sounding board and a fount of knowledge with regard to many of the men, [not just in the Suffolk Regiment] and war memorials in general); Sheila Wright (for advice and allowing me to use information from her excellent books about Drinkstone).

Peg Cameron from Canada (for photographs of James Gill); Lyn Carr from Canada (for a photograph of James Gill's gravestone); David Rose and his sister Judith (for access to family papers, photographs and other items relating to Leonard George Rose); Sheila Coe, Sylvia Lazenby and Rachel (for information about Alfred Harvey); Neil and John Donaghy and Moira Reeve (for giving me access to family papers, photographs and other items relating to William Edwards); Claire and Piers Day (for kindly allowing me access to personal papers, a scrapbook and other items relating to Duncan Vere Webb and his family); Eddie Horrex, Rose Foster and David Bloomfield (for information and a photograph of Percy Bloomfield); Lady Geraldine Hopkins-Jones, Anthony Hopkins-Jones and Benjamin Hargreaves (for a photograph and information relating to Michael Hargreaves and his family); Nigel Rose for photographs and information about George Ernest Rose).

The late John Ottley of Rougham (for sharing information about James Cornish); David Burt (for information about the Seeley family); Jim Gill (for photographs and information about James Gill's medals); Yvonne and Richard Bolt (for photographs of The White House, the Halls' former shop); Jill Carter from Hessett (for sharing her researches about John Whiting); James Munday (for allowing me to take photographs of Treaclebenders, his home, where Alfred Harvey lived); Roger Gillespie (for photographs of Leonard George Rose's medals); Rita Burr of Woolpit Museum (for sharing information about Leonard George Rose); Giles and Daphne Youngs (for delving into archives on my behalf and allowing me to photograph Kopsey Cottage, their home, in which William Edwards lived); Katie and Neil Smith, formerly of Drinkstone House (for allowing me to take photographs of their then home, where the Webb family lived); Peter Batchelor (for information about Arthur Pryke and for photographs of several gravestones and monuments); Derek Cross (for information about George Ernest Rose and for allowing me to photograph No.1 Council Houses, his home, where Percy Bloomfield lived); Edna Gunnett (for allowing me to take photographs of Chesil Cottage, her home, where Percy Bloomfield lived).

Sheila Beswick for her whole-hearted enthusiasm and support for all aspects of the project; Lucy Blake (for allowing access to her mother's scrapbooks); Taff Gillingham (for sharing his knowledge and advice); May Berkouwer and her conservation team (for their interest and outstanding skills in conserving the Arthur Pryke embroidery); the Reverend Ruth Farrell (for all her willing assistance); Laura Smith, freelance journalist formerly of the Bury Free Press (for all her interest);

Steve Rogers of The War Graves Photographic Project (for a photograph of Michael Hargreaves' gravestone); Ben Terrier of the Find a Grave website (for information and a photograph of William Edwards' gravestone); Mick McCann at The British War Graves Archive (for the photograph of Thomas Barker's gravestone); Hannah Rodgers, Assistant Curator at York Army Museum (for help with the story of Albert Smith); Steve Erskine, Assistant Curator of the Green Howards Museum in Richmond, Yorkshire (concerning Alfred Harvey); Robin Jenkins, Leicestershire and Rutland Record Office (for information about Bertie Phillips); Jerry Rudman, Archivist at Uppingham School (for photographs and information about Duncan Vere Webb); Steve Bland, Secretary of the Princess Louise's Kensington Regimental Association (for his interest and support, particularly in the conservation of the Arthur Pryke embroidery); members of the Drinkstone Branch of the Royal British Legion; Google Earth; the National Army Museum; the Imperial War Museum; the Great War Forum - various members, but too many to mention (for sharing their knowledge and researches); members of All Saints' Church; and past and present members of the Drinkstone Village Hall management committee (for support and encouragement).

Councillor Penny Otton (for support and contributions to the project, via Mid-Suffolk District Council and Suffolk County

Council Locality Funds); Drinkstone Educational Trust (for grants to help defray the costs of the project).

Finally, there is an extra-special group of people who deserve my gratitude. First, I should like to thank David Stockwell, a boy two years older than myself, who lived across the road from me in East Ham. He was responsible for firing my interest in the First World War, through speaking enthusiastically about the war poets, as we walked together to and from school in the mid-1960's. Second, my mentor and English teacher, my form master for three years at East Ham Grammar School, who inspired me to be creative and encouraged my love of the English language – Paul Beech has remained a dear and lifelong friend. And I am enormously grateful to my family: to my daughters Ellie and Caitlin who, since they were born, have only known a father with a puzzling pastime; where he has dragged them to cemeteries, monuments and museums in Britain, France and Belgium, spending hours looking into display cases and gazing at lumps of stone. Thank you so much for your patience girls! My deepest thanks, though, go to my wife Louise, not only for her understanding, for her indulgence, for her uncomplaining support and for her belief in me – but also for her help, with research by employing her natural curiosity and enthusiasm, and through her technical knowledge and expertise, *especially* in all things computer-related.

I really don't think I could have done it without such enormous help and support.